That's Not a Toilet!

(True stories of Gross, Scary, and Bizarre College Roommate Experiences)

By Julie Roberts

Eagles Nest Publishing LLC

Copyright 2013

Table of Contents

<u>Dedication</u>

This book is dedicated to my mom and sister; who, after years of hearing my college stories, told me that since I loved telling them so much I should just make a book out of it. Also, I want to thank all of the wonderful people who took the time to share their experiences with me, without you this book never would have been made possible.

Words of Wisdom

One evening during the course of writing this book, I attended a dinner with some old college friends. By this time we had all graduated and moved into adulthood. Gone were the carefree, lazy days of college life. Most of the ladies were married and working, blessed with the joys of motherhood that kept them on call 24 hours a day. This was the first night some of them had gone out on their own in months. Once you've got the responsibilities of the real world, it makes college seem like a vacation. Dinner was spent reminiscing about old times, showing off pictures of adorable new babies, and discussing the strain of potty training. As the evening wound down and we were preparing to leave, one woman commented, "I've had a tough year, and this is the best therapy I've had in a long time." Case in point: friendship is the cheapest form of therapy. A $30 dinner is a lot less expensive than a shrink that charges $100 plus an hour. *Maybe that's why the self-help book craze has skyrocketed; people are too busy and spending less time with their friends, resulting in dire needs for support and acceptance.* So no matter how hectic your life gets, don't forget to stay in touch with the people that matter.

Questions to Ponder...

While writing this book I took the liberty to do four independent polls regarding unique roommate situations. The objective was to see how differently men and women would react in some circumstances. Once again, gender differences became evidently clear. The results from these polls prove that women are designated ass and tear wipers, and men are brave toilet plungers. **Question one**: If one of your roommates was really sick and had to wear a diaper, would you change it for them? *Remember the Golden Rule: Do onto others as you would have others do onto you.*

Results

Men	Women
99% no	60% no
1% yes	40% yes

This goes to show that if you live with guys and need help with your incontinence, it's best to get a private nurse or move back home. And as for the women who said no, let's hope they don't plan on becoming mothers any time soon. Hey, a diaper is a diaper, no matter what size it comes in.

Question two: If you came back to your dorm and found one of your roommates sitting on the couch crying, what would you do?

Results

Men: The majority of men replied: "I'd say, 'what's up' or 'hey man want a beer?' The thought of offering a shoulder to cry on did not occur to most of them. I'll never forget the reaction of my friend Matt, one of the first guys I polled. We had stopped at an ice cream parlor on a warm summer day, relaxing in the sun, and I thought this was a prime opportunity to catch him at a sensitive moment. *Wishful thinking on my part.* "So tell me Matt, what would you do if you found one of your buddies crying on the couch?" There was a pause, and I waited for his sympathetic side to emerge. First his face contorted, he pondered for a moment, then raised his hand up with a moving declaration: "I'll tell you what I wouldn't do. I WOULD NOT ... (Brief dramatic pause) go comfort him!"

I even asked a young seminarian this question. I thought since maybe he was studying to become a priest he would react more gently than most guys. Hah! No such chance. Here is what he said: "I might offer him a beer, but I wouldn't go console him. I would think there was something wrong with him, guys don't cry in public!" Even men of God have their consoling limits. My own uncle put it perfectly when he said, "It depends on what he was crying over. But would I go over to him? No. Guys don't do that." Let's hope that all crying men have a mom or girlfriend they could call for some nurturing, because their buddies would not be up to the task.

Women: Almost every woman questioned answered, "I would ask them what's wrong." Now that's friendship! If their crying roommate left the scene, about half of the women said they would follow them to find out what happened. Come on, we all know that if someone is crying and takes off, they usually are *hoping* to be chased after. *Remember that men the next time you see a woman cry.* Why else would they be crying out in the open? They want to be caught! Strangely, no woman said they would offer their friend a beer. Go figure.

Case in point: Your very own, "That's Not a Toilet!" author was once faced with this exact situation while in college. While interviewing for this book, one of my former roommates was kind enough to remind me of a time when I came back from class and found her sitting on her bed crying. "Waaaah!" Being the caring friend that I am; I sat down, patted her on the back, and asked if something was wrong. Looking back that was a dumb question, it was obvious something was wrong or she wouldn't be opening Niagara Falls on her bed.

She told me something about her asshole professor and a stressful class. She feared she might fail the course. My response? Not too nurturing, I was uncomfortable and looking for an exit. "Well, I don't really know what to do in these situations, so I'll be in the kitchen if you need me." And I got up and left the room to go make dinner. Hey, I was hungry.

Question three: Have you ever seen those CPR posters that give step-by-step illustrated instructions on how to save a life? Well during the course of this book I saw a similar poster taped up in a health class. But instead of pictured CPR directions, this poster gave step-by-step instructions on how to give someone a rectal injection using a drug called Diastat. My first thought was: "What the hell is this?" Too embarrassed to ask anyone about it, after a quick Internet research I discovered that it had a crucial purpose: Rectal Diastat (dye-ah-stat) is the best known treatment for acute repetitive seizures (bout or cluster of seizures with retention of consciousness in between seizures). It has a short duration of action when given intravenously but works immediately when administered rectally. In this case, back door entry is the best way to go.

So this got me thinking, and here is your question to ponder: If one of your roommates was having a prolonged seizure and needed a rectal injection, would you give it to them?

Men	Women
70% no	20% no
30% yes	80% yes

Most common male response: "I'd say, 'Nice knowing you buddy." How heartless! Let's hope they would change their mind and put the gloves on if ever faced with that situation. Best female response: "Yeah! Cause if I had to stick something up *their ass* to make *them* feel better, I would." Think about it, it's easier than sticking it up your own ass.

Question four: If your significant other plugged the toilet, would you plunge it for them? While living away from mom and dad, college is a time for couples to share unlimited time together, often having sleepovers and extended visits. This next poll was based off of a true story. Bill had recently starting dating Kathy, and one morning after a dozen beers he woke up in her apartment with terrible beer shits. After relieving himself, to his horror he saw the toilet was plugged. "Fuck!" Bill cried in despair.

He glanced around frantically looking for a plunger, but there was none to be found. Kathy noticed he had been in there a long time and called out to ask if he was alright. "Uh, do you have a plunger?" Bill asked sheepishly. She didn't. So Bill did what he had to do, he went home and let

Kathy deal with his delivery. *What a gentleman huh?* The surprising part of this story is that Kathy actually kept dating Bill for a while after cleaning his mess. Maybe there was some kind of fecal fetish going on…?

Men 100% yes	**Women** 10% yes
	90% no

The large discrepancy between and male and female responses shows men see plunging as another male duty; like cleaning the gutters or mowing the lawn. A male relative of mine said it clearly when he answered, "Of course I would plunge it for her. I poo, she poos." Just to get a larger age sample, I even asked my 85 year old grandmother this question. I thought perhaps after 50 years of marriage she wouldn't mind performing such a chore for her spouse. Her response: "I'd tell him why don't you plunge it yourself! You plugged it, you plunge it." Sounds fair to me.

Final Thoughts

So do you think you're a good person, the kind who will be supportive and considerate of their friends' feelings and needs? Would you stand by them in times of heartache and suffering? Or would you turn your back and walk away? Well consider these questions and ask yourself: what would *I do* in those situations? Comfort, ignore, wipe, inject, plunge, or laugh? Something to analyze your true character...

Hygiene Issues

College is filled with all kinds of educational experiences outside the classroom. Students learn about relationships, personal growth, adult responsibility, and in some cases, basic hygiene concepts.

Merry Christmas

Freshmen often begin their college adventure living with people they have never met before. This can be a great learning experience as they learn how to share space, accommodate individual needs, and accept others' different living habits and styles. All of us have our own unique personal tastes and ways of taking care of ourselves (example: some like to shower at night, others are morning washers.) But certain students end up with roommates that have particularly low hygiene standards, and this can lead to uncomfortable situations. Such was the case with Becky, who, because of one roommate's stench, ended up resenting her own sense of smell.

Becky lived in an all-female dorm along with three other girls. She got along well with two of them, but the third one, Amy, had the worst hygiene problems they had ever encountered. What was so bad you ask? For starters, she smelled like an ashtray. It's a common fact in college that after you come back from a party you usually reek of smoke and alcohol (a trip to the shower is often a top priority once sobriety sets in).

But in Amy's case, she would go out partying at least four nights a week, while only bothering to shower about twice a week. The smoky stench would linger on her for days on end. Becky and her other roommates began living with a constant odor of B.O. and smoke. Even neighboring guys, who were used to the smell of dirty laundry and moldy pizza, would tell them that their room reeked.

Pity those who sat by Amy in class. She would wake up, roll out of bed, and go to class in the same clothes she had on the night before, without even bothering to brush her teeth! It's amazing this girl even found people who were willing to hang out with her. Either they had no sense of smell or were too drunk most of the time to even notice her odor. Alcohol has a way of dulling the sensory system.

The girls didn't know a nice way to approach Amy about her stench. After all, is there really any "nice" way to tell someone they reek? By the end of the first semester they had had enough and decided to take action. As Christmas time came around, they came up with a creative plan: why not give Amy the gift of good hygiene? So they got her a card, donated $5.00 a piece, and wrote a note saying, "Please use for soap, shampoo, toothbrush, and a box of douche."

Instead of being thankful, Amy actually took offense! She ran down the hall and ranted to their RA, Auburn, about what they had done to her. A roommate meeting was called, and Auburn told them, "Ladies, hygiene is a personal issue, and it's not appropriate to interfere with someone else's private habits. You need to apologize to Amy for being so rude." Rude! Amy

15

forced them to live with their noses plugged and they were the ones who were being rude? Damn that Liberal RA approach. So after a sarcastic apology, they were forced to wallow in her stink for the rest of the school year. They used Amy's Christmas gift to buy room freshener and scented candles.

Selective Bathing

Every person has their own ritual for bathing. Some start out by washing their feet first, then moving up to their body till it's time to shampoo. Others begin with washing their hair and then lathering their way down to the toes. For some students (especially females) showers and tubs are filled with a variety of shampoos, conditioners, body washes, back scrubs, foot scrubs, razors, etc.

Guys' showers tend to be simpler, usually containing just the basic necessities of soap and shampoo. No matter where you begin to wash your body or what brand of cleanser you use, rest assured you will be fresh once you exit the shower...right?

In most cases, that is correct. But there are rare instances when the water will fail. People can find ways to shower and still be at least partially dirty. Before starting college, Chloe was excited about getting a new roommate. She thought it would be a great opportunity to get to know someone new, but her excitement was soon diminished once she met her roommate, Michelle. Right after moving in the dorm, it didn't take long for Chloe to discover that Michelle did not keep her hygiene up to par.

Michelle didn't shower for the first three days after they moved in, and Chloe could smell her from across the room. So it was a huge relief when she saw Michelle grab her bathrobe and head into the bathroom. Once she heard the shower running Chloe did a little happy dance around the room. "Maybe she just wasn't feeling well the first few days," Chloe reasoned with herself. She wanted to give Michelle the benefit of the doubt. "I hope now she'll make this a daily habit."

Since it was her first shower in days, Chloe figured Michelle would take her time and really scrub away the oil and dirt; so she was shocked when Michelle exited the bathroom after only two minutes. "Gosh Michelle, that sure was quick," Chloe couldn't keep the surprise from her voice. "Oh, that's cause today was my hair shower, next time I'll wash and shave." Michelle answered as she disappeared into the bedroom.

Chloe remained in shock. "Hair shower? I must have heard her wrong," she thought. "I'm sorry Michelle, did you say today was *your hair shower*?"

she called out in disbelief. "Yeah, I just washed my hair today. I never wash everything at once, I get too bored. So now that my hair is clean I'll wash my body next time," Michelle answered through the door. She made it sound like it was perfectly normal to be only half-clean after bathing.

Chloe still couldn't believe what she was hearing. "Let me get this straight," she said when Michelle came out of the bedroom. "Today you washed your hair, and nothing else?" She couldn't keep the disgust out of her voice. "Well I didn't use soap or anything, but I still got clean from the water!" Michelle said defensively. "I find that my hair and skin dry out easily, so I don't wash them every time I shower. I'll do one or the other, and it works out better that way." *Better to have greasy hair than a fishy cooch.*

And so it went on like this for the rest of the year. Michelle continued to shower every few days, and she would announce beforehand which type of shower it would be. "I'm washing my legs and feet today," she'd declare as went into the bathroom. She never saw the abnormality of her own behavior, even after word got around and people would ask her, "Hey Michelle, what kind of shower is it today?" The only good thing about her odd behavior was that Michelle didn't hog the bathroom. Unlike most female roommates, Chloe never had to force Michelle out of the bathroom. Quite the contrary, she wanted her to *stay in it*, at least long enough to scrub her ass.

Is That a Tampon?

Have you ever heard of the term, "ignorance is bliss?" I know this saying to be true, because sometimes it's best not to know something than learning disturbing news. And you never really know someone until you live with them. The main reason roommate relations move from sweet to sour is because people learn too much about each other. Someone who appears to be a nice, sane, ordinary person can turn out to be nuttier than a fruitcake behind closed doors. There are people in our society who ought to be institutionalized, yet they continue to live freely and elude the system.

If you are stuck living with someone who's missing a screw or two, the cloud of ignorance can protect you. For some people, if they knew half the things their roommates secretly did, they'd end up either sleeping in shifts or with a baseball bat. That's why it's sometimes better to stay in the dark about things; it lets you keep the illusion that everything and everyone around you is safe and normal.

Nina experienced this firsthand during her sophomore year, when her head was finally forced out of the clouds of roommate harmony. She had moved into the dorm with two others, Diane and Rachel. And at first, everything seemed fine. She had met Diane freshmen year and they had agreed to be roommates. Since they needed another person, Diane found Rachel to be their third roommate. Even though she had never met Rachel, Nina was confidant things would be fine. She trusted Diane's opinion, and when she had talked to Rachel on the phone over the summer she had sounded like a pleasant, sweet person. *Don't most serial killers appear nice before they boil their victims and store them in the fridge?*

Summer passed and with fall came move-in day. The girls settled into their room and at first it was the honeymoon stage. *The brief period when everyone is on their best behavior and pretends to be polite and considerate.* Rachel appeared to be a friendly, cheerful person and was eager to bond as roommates with activities such as eating together, watching movies, staying up late talking, etc. Nina thought she had lucked out with another great roommate.

Unfortunately, it didn't take long for her to realize that her new friend might not be as she appeared. First came the odor. Nina and Diane began noticing a peculiar smell around their room. In the beginning they didn't know where it was coming from, but pretty soon they figured out that Rachel was the culprit. Her body gave off this sickening scent that lingered in the air even when she was out of the room. This was puzzling because Rachel did shower every night, yet her odor was still nauseating.

It was a weird smell, not like typical body odor, and she would try to cover it up by marinating herself with perfume every day. *A piece of advice: when you already reek, perfume or cologne won't make it any better, it just adds more layers to the stench.* The girls knew they had a problem on their hands, but they weren't sure how to handle it. Hygiene is never an easy subject to address with people, especially when you wish to stay on good terms.

Meanwhile the smell seemed to get worse. Diane summed it up best by saying, "Not to be gross or anything, but she smells like rotting crotch." It was suspected that Rachel was a non-soap believer, thinking that by the grace of God water alone would get her clean. She did read the bible every day, but maybe she skipped the part when Jesus washed his disciples' feet. She almost never did laundry, so it didn't help that she was always wearing dirty clothes.

They decided not to broach the subject of Rachel's hygiene. As sophomores they were experienced enough to know that that would only lead to roommate conflict. And when you're living in an environment small enough to breed claustrophobics, it's usually better to keep the peace whenever possible. A little smell was better than having a roommate hate you, so they just bought some Febreze, opened the windows, and put up with it. Whenever

Rachel was gone their dorm got a nice spray down, but the smell always came back.

Meanwhile it became obvious that hygiene was not the only one of Rachel's problems. Although publicly she kept a friendly demeanor, she also had a dark, moody side that was kept behind closed doors. She would take on a, "don't look at me, don't talk to me," attitude and spend half the day sleeping.

Nina and Diane thought it was another case of someone slipping through the cracks of the mental health system. Once they get to college, some students who are on medication stop taking it, since Mommy and Daddy aren't there to place it on their tongue. This usually leads them to eventually being sent home from school or a trip to the psych ward. *A piece of advice on medication: if you're prescribed it, take it, and if you need it, see a doctor!*

You might think the girls were being too hard on Rachel. So what if she is a little smelly and moody right? That doesn't mean the girl has any serious issues. Well let me ask you this: What would you think if someone kept soiled tampons in their desk drawer? That's right used, dirty, tampons: now pick your jaw off the floor.

Nina made this atrocious discovery one afternoon when she was searching for a pencil. Opening up Rachel's desk drawer to grab one, instead she found several dried out, bloody tampons stashed among the clutter. "Is that what I think it is? No, no, it can't be...oh my God it is!" Her bubble of ignorant bliss was instantly popped: it was now confirmed that she was living with a complete psycho. Who knew what else this girl was capable of? And Nina was the one sleeping right above her! She would be the most vulnerable for attack if Rachel decided to collect someone else's blood.

After a moment of shock, Nina closed the drawer and back-stepped out of the room. One thing was for sure; there was no way she was going to tell Rachel about her discovery, she felt it was safer that way to keep pretending all was well. But she did show Diane the first chance she got, and Diane's expression of disgust and shock was worth a thousand bucks.

Thank-God there was only a few weeks left in the semester. The girls kept up their false display of normalcy. If Rachel knew her cover was blown, she might start leaving tampons everywhere or perhaps begin sacrificing small animals in their room.

One thing was sure; this did explain why there was always a foul odor lingering around. If you've never smelled a rotting used tampon, don't try it. The girls managed to survive the year without injury, but their roommate innocence was gone forever.

As for Rachel, she went on to finish her college degree, maintaining a 4.0 GPA and graduating with honors. This goes to show, you don't have to be sane to be smart. It is unknown whether or not her odor ever improved, or if she kept her tampon collection. Let's just hope her future roommates stayed out of her desk.

RA Science

Resident Assistants, more commonly known as RA's, are a strong presence in dormitory life. They have the difficult job of supervising residents with issues such as alcohol violations, roommate conflicts, fire drills, and being on call for emergencies. In order to be an RA one must go through an intense interviewing and training process. It takes a special person to be an RA, someone who is open-minded, caring, and thriving for that free room and board that they receive with the job.

One of the great things about having an RA in the dorm is that they can help students deal with issues that they don't feel comfortable handling on their own. After all, the RA is sort of like the resident babysitter. A go-to mediator for roommate conflict; an objective third party who tries to see all sides of a situation. There are some instances, however, that can cause even the most experienced RA to wither in shock.

Imaginary Shower

As an RA in a female dorm, Sue was accustomed to dealing with petty squabbles. Girls tend to be catty and fight over little things more than guys do. And that was expected, especially from the freshmen that were straight out of home. Sue spent a lot of time the first semester mediating roommate issues, trying to negotiate and find common ground, but nothing prepared her for what she was about to encounter.

One day some girls came to see her and said they had a problem they wanted to talk about. Their roommate, Katie, had major hygiene issues and stunk so bad that they couldn't stand being near her. It turned out that Katie was involved in an army program on campus, and would often come back dirty and sweaty from the exercise and drills. This wouldn't have been a problem if she cleaned up right away, but Katie seemed to like her smell and pretended that the shower didn't exist. After her training she would leave her sweaty clothes on the rest of the day; and her smell lingered with her.

As the RA, it was up to Sue to talk to Katie about this and explain to her why her roommates were upset. She did something called *care-fronting*; which meant addressing a situation in a calm and non-judgmental manner. "I'm sure you want to get along with your roommates, but your infrequent bathing is making them upset. If you made an effort to shower more regularly, this would really help the situation." Katie agreed to shower at least four times a week, and Sue felt confident that she had resolved the issue.

A few days later, the girls came back, this time with another shocking scenario. Katie must have had a shower phobia, because instead of getting in, she was only pretending to shower. That's right, pretending. How does one pretend to shower? Well she would go in the bathroom, turn on the shower, and then walk out a few minutes later in a bathrobe with a towel wrapped around her head.

They soon noticed, however, that Katie was never wet after these so-called showers. She would simply turn on the shower, wait a few minutes, and come out in her robe. Her roommates were flabbergasted. If you're going to bother getting naked and turning on the water, why not just get in?

So once again Sue had to care-front Katie about her hygiene habits: "Your roommates have again expressed concerns to me that you are not showering regularly like you agreed to." Katie's response: "They must not be around when I shower. I get in there at least every other day." She said that with a straight face. Hmmmm ...With the smell of body odor and greasy hair encompassed around her, Sue wondered if this girl really believed that her *pretend* showers were real. Unfortunately, Sue had to break the news to her roommates that they were out of luck. She had done all she could do, and unless they were willing to scrub Katie down themselves, they would be forced to live with her stench and imaginary showers for the rest of the year. Perhaps Katie was experimenting with a new self-defense technique: keep away the enemy with your stench.

Birthday Blues

As a student living in the dorms, there are certain rules that one has to abide by. (Smoke only in designated rooms, no wild parties or underage drinking, etc.) Because college students are notorious for starting fires, certain things such as lava lamps and candles are often prohibited. Such was the case in Stacey's dorm. Stacey was approaching her 19th birthday, and her friends decided to throw a little party for her, despite the *no candle* rule...

Thinking it would cause no harm, they waited in her room with a cake and had one friend go downstairs and wait for Stacey to get back from class. "Oh won't she be surprised?" they anticipated with excitement. Little did they know that another surprise was brewing. As soon as Stacey walked in the room, the smoke detector started going off.

What would become of them? This was against the rules! Of course the noise got the attention of their RA, Brenda, who came down to inspect. Brenda was the type who loved being in a power position. She often took pleasure in writing people up for minor offenses such as playing your music too loud. Luckily, Brenda was in a generous mood that day.

When she saw that birthday candles had started the raucous, she smirked and said, "Well your birthday present is, I'm not going to write you up." What a big heart Brenda, just wait and see if you get a cake on your birthday…

No Sweat

Perspiration is a fact of life for everybody, and it varies uniquely for each person. Issues such as body chemistry, climate, and physical activity all play a role in how much someone sweats. Not only is the wetness annoying and embarrassing; the odor will force others to keep their distance. Fortunately, modern science allows us to fight the battle of the glands. Anti-perspirant deodorants and sprays are designed to keep the wetness at bay.

Certain people are born to sweat; it doesn't matter where they are or what they're wearing or doing, that annoying liquid will find its way out of their pores. Then there are the lucky few people that merely *glow*, they could do a marathon in Death Valley and still keep their clothes dry (and possibly die of heat exhaustion.) It's important that we're aware of our bodies' sweat habits so we can keep it under control. A daily shower and dose of deodorant is usually all it takes, but some people see their bodies as being above the disgraceful act of sweat.

Such was the case with Laura. Like the problems with most hygiene-deficient people, Laura did not believe in daily bathing, but she did manage to find time to exercise each day. For most people, a shower is soon taken after a sweaty workout session.

But as her roommate soon discovered, Laura was the exception. She would work out, come back sweaty and flushed, and not shower for the rest of the day. Her lingering sweat smell was impossible to ignore, and her roommate Natalie had to find a way to address it.

One day after Laura returned from the gym, Natalie asked her why she never showered after a workout. Laura simply replied, "Because I don't sweat." Don't sweat? She said it as if she was saying, "Don't smoke," like it was perfectly normal and natural. "What do you mean you don't sweat?" Natalie asked in disbelief. "You bust your ass everyday at aerobics!" "Yeah, but I'm lucky. My body gets hot, but I still never sweat. I can't even remember the last time I wore deodorant," Laura said proudly.

Needless to say, Natalie was disgusted and didn't know what to do. On one hand, she liked Laura and didn't want to hurt her feelings, but at the same time she was grossed out by her false sense of cleanliness. She decided to take a subtle approach and link bathing to something Laura could relate to: exercise. "You know Laura, I read somewhere that hot water is great for your muscles after a workout; you might want to try that after aerobics tomorrow," Natalie tried to keep the desperation out of her voice. Laura's response? "I don't sweat, so I don't need to."

Failed attempt... shit. Natalie decided not to broach the subject again; some people are just too nice. She should have said, "Look girl, you'd better get your ass in the shower, cause you reek!" Laura continued her daily workout routine, still only making it to the shower about once a week. There was hope though, being unsure of what to major in, Laura was thinking about becoming a nurse. Hopefully she would eventually take an anatomy class, which should prove to her that she does indeed have sweat glands. Sorry sweetie, as much as you want to deny it, your shit stinks and your pits drip.

Dirty Hands

It is a well-known fact that hand washing is the number one way to prevent the spread of disease. From early age on children are taught to wash their hands before eating, and most importantly, after using the bathroom. Does this scene sound familiar? Little Johnny flushes the toilet, and Mom calls out, "Don't forget to wash your hands!" Sitting down for dinner, "Did you wash your hands first?" Although these frequent reminders can get annoying, they are necessary to implant the need for sanitation in a child's mind.

A little fear doesn't hurt either; just turn on the TV and watch a segment about the dangers of raw meat. Certain meats can contain such fun bacteria as Escherichia coli, or more commonly known as E-coli, which, if it enters the body, can give the lucky recipient a long period of bloody diarrhea and abdominal cramps. Why do you think restaurants have those "Employees must wash hands" signs put up in every bathroom? If someone gets shit on their hands after wiping their ass; they can spread it to the food and into the mouths of poor unknowing customers, yum. ☺

After years of parental reminders and learning about germs in school, hopefully by the time one enters college they are seasoned hand-washers. They don't need to be reminded to wash their hands after shitting or wiping their nose. But there are always exceptions to the rule...

As a freshman, Melissa moved into the dorms with three other roommates. Everything started off fine as the girls settled into college life, but they soon noticed something peculiar about Melissa. She never seemed to wash her hands. Whenever she used the bathroom they'd hear the toilet flush, but the sink would never be turned on. She would simply wipe her ass and walk out, taking her waste with her. Gross! This meant that Melissa's pee and poop were being passed onto whatever she touched or ate.

She kept a lot of food in the room, and the best part was when she would use the bathroom, not wash, and then have a snack. *Her roommates made sure to never get their food mixed up with hers.* Melissa must have been absent or sleeping on the days they taught about germs in grade school, or maybe she was raised in a home that didn't believe in soap. Either way it was a known fact that when the bathroom fan went on someone was taking a dump; and after finishing their business they flushed, sprayed some glade, wash, then quickly closed the door behind them.

Melissa remembered to flush and spray, but she never turned on the sink. *It's interesting that she cared about the smell but not the germs.* Her hands were always bone dry after exiting the bathroom. In desperation her roommates put a big bottle of hand-sanitizer on the bathroom counter, hoping she would at least use that. No such luck.

After a few weeks the bottle still had not been used, and the girls were constantly spraying Lysol everywhere to counter Melissa's trail of germs. Soon their entire room smelled like a hospital. They finally approached their RA, Molly, and told her their concerns about Melissa's lack of hand washing. Molly had her doubts. "Are you sure she's not washing guys? I mean, how do you know if she's always got the door closed?" "Because we can hear everything that she does in there, and the sink never goes on after she flushes!" They replied with frustration. "All right then, if you really think that there is a problem, I'll do a roommate meeting with all you." Molly offered.

The next day they all gathered in their dorm for a "Roommate Negotiation." *It's like marriage counseling only much cheaper.* At first, Molly went over the basics; giving phone messages, no crazy guests, have a cleaning schedule, etc. Then a brief pause, and Molly said, "As you know, dorms are a breeding ground for germs because there are so many people living in a small space. Are all of you keeping clean and washing your hands regularly?" "That's so exaggerated!" Melissa said defensively. "I hardly *ever* wash my hands and I don't get sick." She made it sound as if it were something to be proud of! "Well, we could get sick!" Her roomies shouted back. "Whenever you don't wash you walk around spreading your crap everywhere. We don't want to be touching your shit!"

Melissa just shrugged. "I don't have to wash my hands if I don't want to." The RA then tried to reason with her, "You know Melissa, it really is unsanitary for you and your roommates if you don't"...blah blah. The rest of her speech might as well have been told to a chimp. *Of course a chimp could probably be taught to wash their hands.*

The meeting ended without an ounce of success. If anything, it even motivated Melissa to stay dirty. She continued to avoid soap like the plague. As for her roommates, they cleaned so much you could practically eat off of the toilet, and washed their hands more than a butt doctor. Let's hope Melissa wasn't planning on entering the food industry, or else an outbreak might result.

Dish Wars

One of the most common and stupid arguments among college roommates is about dirty dishes. Many students are under the false impression that if they just wait long enough, their dishes will either magically disappear or find a way to clean themselves. And the funny thing is, no one ever knows whose they are. Excuses such as, "Those aren't mine," or "I didn't use that bowl," are commonly heard. Each residence must be inhabited by a dish phantom that just comes in, eats, and leaves the messy dishes behind. As a result, they are often left unclaimed and soiled for days, weeks, or even months. This can lead to some pretty vicious arguments; what I have come to refer to as "Dish Wars." Countries are willing to go to war over oil, land, and imaginary weapons of mass destruction, while our best and brightest will fight to the death over what's left in the sink.

If You Can Wash That ...

During her sophomore year Maryanne shared an apartment with four other girls. It wasn't a good arrangement. Her roommates found countless ways to annoy her, and she spent as much time away from the apartment as possible. Those four were extremely lazy, never attempting to do basic tasks such as cleaning the bathroom or taking out the trash. These were all things that irritated Maryanne, but dishes were at the top of the list.

Out of the five people living in that apartment, Maryanne was the only one who bothered to wash her dishes. Her roommates would let their dishes pile up in the sink for weeks at a time. If it weren't for Maryanne, everybody probably would have been eating off of the floor. That really pissed her off. Why should she get stuck washing their mess?

One of the first rules of relationships, no matter what type, is open communication. Did she try talking to them about the problem? You bet. First the nice approach, "Could you guys please remember to wash your dishes when you're done?" No luck. Then the pleading method, "Please take care of your dishes, it's really gross when we let them pile up like that." Tough shit. Followed by frustration; "I'm getting sick of this you guys, wash your damn dishes!"

All of this fell on deaf ears. Her roommates always claimed that they were washing their dishes and they didn't know whose those were in the sink. They even tried placing the blame on Maryanne; "It's probably your friends that aren't washing their dishes when they come over." Not likely, Maryanne almost never had people at the apartment; she was ashamed of its slovenly appearance.

This dirty dish cycle went on for months. But every person has their breaking point, and Maryanne eventually met hers. One evening after a long day of classes, all she wanted to do at home was eat and relax. Sounds easy right? But when she entered the kitchen she encountered a problem.

There were no clean dishes, and everything was piled high in the sink, creating a smelly and ugly sight. Aaah! That's when Maryanne lost her last shred of patience; and the newfound fury quickly brought on a drive for revenge. What would it be? Toss a lipstick in with their laundry? Bake up laxative-laced brownies? No, she wanted a more direct approach. Grabbing a hefty garbage bag, she loaded up everything from the sink. "This will teach those lazy bitches," she thought with vengeance.

The next morning her roommates discovered a nice surprise in the bathroom. Left in the shower was a garbage bag full of dirty dishes, along with a note that read, "If you can wash your cooter, then you can wash your damn dishes!" When you think about it, cleaning one's crotch is similar to dish washing. Both involve warm water, soap, and the risk of bugs if you wait too long. Since Maryanne would no longer be their dish bitch, the girls reluctantly washed their hefty present.

Even though this did not put an end to their roommate squabbles, from then on they were a little better about doing the dishes. As for Maryanne, she continued to use her apartment just as a place to sleep and bathe. She prayed her next living situation would be an improvement. Let's hope her next roommates washed both their cooters and their dishes, or else they might find a dirty gift in the shower.

Dish Strategy

It's general knowledge that men live differently than women, and it's usually easy to tell whether or not a place is inhabited with females. Certain clues can always be found such as framed pictures, living plants, scented candles, etc. And if the decorating doesn't clue you in, all you need to do is look in the refrigerator. Have you ever studied the contents of a bachelor's fridge? That's the first thing I like to do when I enter a guy's place for the first time. It always amazes me how little they have (beer, ketchup, spoiled milk, possibly some left over pizza.)

Nine times out of ten there is barely enough food to feed a mouse, yet the guys still can't lose their pot bellies. Hey, that's how fast food stays in business. Despite the lack of food and cooking, guys still manage to have their own dish wars, although they never take it as personally as the women do; Thank God. John discovered this fact during his sophomore year, living off campus with four other guys.

Like Maryanne, John got stuck with some of the laziest people imaginable. They each had their own slovenly habits. For example, Andy, a victim of self-inflicted obesity, weighed close to 400lbs. He would drink several 2-liter bottles of pop each day while beached in front of the TV. Of course he never bothered to throw the bottles away; after he was done he would just toss them on the floor to be left untouched.

Another roommate, Kyle, found his own way to avoid ever cleaning the bathroom. There were two bathrooms in their house and Kyle would shower downstairs but use the upstairs bathroom for peeing and crapping. Because he showered downstairs, he claimed he didn't have to clean the upstairs bathroom. *Personally I'd rather have a dirty shower than a shit-laced toilet.*

None of the guys bothered to clean. Whenever the garbage would get full, they would just let it overflow, continuing to pile crap around it. *Maybe they thought the garbage man made house calls.* John tried waiting to see if anyone else would take care of it, but eventually he would cave in and take it out. That's one of the main issues with college cleaning; whoever ends up doing it once is usually stuck with that designated role.

Fortunately, John was an easy-going guy, a good trait to have for college living. He could deal with the pop bottles strewn around the living room and a bathroom filled with mold and pubic hair, but what really got to him was the......drum roll please ......DISHES! That's right. If people aren't willing to empty the trash or clean the tub, odds are they're not going to bother doing their dishes.

Now John was not very confrontational, so he didn't try bitching at them to solve the problem. *It wouldn't have worked anyway; guys tend to just tune each other out, while girls will bitch back and forth till they can't even remember what they were bitching about.* Instead, he came up with a more strategic solution.

John began storing basic utensils in his room. When he needed something he would use it, wash it, and then hide it back in the closet. He knew his roommates wouldn't catch on to what he was doing. Guys aren't very observant, one of them would have to set his nuts on fire and run around screaming before anyone would take notice. John figured it was only a matter of time before the others totally ran out of dishes and were forced to wash them.

Sure enough, soon the cupboards were bare and the sink was overflowing with a week's worth of dishes. But it turns out that John's roommates were even lazier than he gave them credit for. Whenever they needed something they would just take it out of the sink, wash, use, then dump it back. Whatever was on the bottom remained there till they moved out, disgusting. Even though the outcome wasn't what he hoped, John was still pleased. Another tip: if you can't reason with them, it's better to outsmart them. The dishes were still dirty, but at least he only had to wash his own.

The Good, The Bad, and The Disgusting

What separates man from the apes? Apes often have higher standards of living.

Flock of Seagulls

For most college students, summer is a time to get away from the grind of studying and the work of campus life. It allows many a chance to work and pay back some of the debt that they've accumulated in the past year by waiting tables, flipping burgers, etc. Of course, some jobs have unexpected burdens...

Instead of going home for the summer, Betty took a job working as a waitress at a summer amusement park. The park provided dormitory housing for its summer employees, and Betty got assigned a roommate named Casey. Right from the start, she knew it wasn't going to be a match made in heaven.

Casey wasn't what you would call a "considerate" roommate. Casey's belongings overtook everything, leaving only a small corner for Betty. She didn't believe in closets or hangers, her clothes were scattered all about. Despite these annoyances, Betty kept her cool. It's usually better to keep the peace than have a war with your roommate, but she soon discovered that there are some things you just can't ignore.

Everyone has their passions, and Casey's was animal rights. To say Casey was a nature freak would be an understatement. She believed all life was precious and would rather live with a spider than kill it. Soon she began finding dying seagulls outside and insisted on saving them. She once climbed into a full dumpster to rescue one seagull, only to have security find and kill it later. That didn't deter her, and she kept searching for injured gulls.

One night Betty came back after a long day at work, exhausted and ready to crawl into bed. Low and behold, a squawking noise greeted her as she entered the room, and she screamed with fright. "Shhh!" Casey lunged off her bed, clasped her hand over Betty's mouth, and slammed the door behind her. "Somebody will hear you!" Betty pulled back and stared wide-mouthed with shock at what she saw. "Casey...there is a seagull in our room." "I know." "No, Casey there is a seagull in our ROOM." "I know...I..." "WHY IS THERE A SEAGULL IN OUR ROOM!" Betty lost her cool. The pent-up frustration had reached the surface. "Because they'd kill it if I turned it in!" Casey stated.

Just then the bird started hopping towards Betty's belongings; looking for a place to crap. She shooed it away. "Hey, be nice!" Casey reprimanded. "Be nice?" Betty's mind reeled. Never in all of her life, in all of her craziest dreams, had she thought that she would be living with a seagull!

"Casey, it's a garbage bird! And it's in our room!" Betty fumed. "It won't be for long," Casey insisted. "I just want to take it home with me when the job's over." Betty couldn't believe it. Casey wanted to keep this bird ...this bottom-feeder with wings...this large, smelly, molting rat with a beak home with her! "Casey, you're not leaving for another two weeks! And what if we get caught with it? You know we're not supposed to have animals! They will fire us and we'll lose our bonuses!"

"No they won't. Ms. Jenkins knows we have it, and she agrees with me." Ms. Jenkins was one of the gatekeepers of the dorm, a kind of a dorm-mom and rule enforcer. It turned out that Casey had pulled a heartstring-number on poor Ms. Jenkins. She came to her crying about the bird, saying that she would take care of it and that it wouldn't hurt anything.

Betty was drained, both physically and mentally. Too exhausted to fight anymore, she agreed that Casey could keep the bird as long as it was kept hidden and never touched her stuff. Good thing Casey was creative; she made a small birdcage by putting a laundry basket over it. Over the course of the next two weeks, that is where the poor bird remained; being fed by food pushed through the holes in the basket. What a tortuous rescue. Soon Casey moved out, taking her new friend with her. However, the odor in the room became almost unbearable. A detestable stench of seagull excrement filled the air. Betty spent her remaining days at work sleeping in a friend's room.

As for Casey the seagull savior, Betty never talked to her again. She did wonder what happened to that poor seagull though. After spending two weeks living under a laundry basket and then forced to move in with Casey, no doubt it wished that it had just been left to die.

Going Natural

College is a time when young adults are often inspired to roll up their sleeves and pitch in a hand at saving the world. The Liberal atmosphere on campus encourages students to expand their horizons and reach out to others. Most campuses offer many opportunities to join organizations and volunteer for various causes such as soup kitchens, nursing homes, mentoring, fundraising, tutoring, etc. There are numerous ways students can help their fellow man. Of course, saving the world begins at home. There are many things one can do on their own to help make the world a better place such as recycling pop cans and turning off the faucet.

Some things, however, just aren't worth the sacrifice, no matter how beneficial they may be to the environment. Kim discovered this her sophomore year while living with Connie. On the surface Connie had seemed like a sound, rational person. She was very involved in a campus green group and adamant about recycling everything possible. Kim didn't mind this; she wanted to do her part to help the Earth. She had no idea how far Connie was willing to go, but she soon learned the depth of her roommate's environmental devotion.

Connie was enrolled in a class about feminism in society, the kind that encouraged women to step out of their traditional roles and fight the oppression that man has bestowed on them. One of her assignments was to read a book about female empowerment, which focused greatly on the incredible strength of female genitalia. Which, when you think about it, does having amazing power. Can you imagine a penis managing to push out a baby?

After reading it Connie saw her vagina in a completely new light. It was not just a site for reproduction and sexual ecstasy, but also a source of ecological hazard. This book opened her eyes to a fresh vision; Connie no longer saw her period as just a monthly annoyance and pregnancy detector. She discovered that the methods used to control it were also a link to pollution.

Don't be fooled by their innocent appearance, pads and tampons are a hazard to nature; a clog to toilets and nasty addition to waste dumps. Take a stand ladies! The book said women should do away with them and use more natural methods, things that are reusable and would not add more to landfills. Connie was intrigued by this idea and announced that from then on she was going to go *all natural*.

How does a woman go all natural and not appear to be hemorrhaging through her pants? After a trip to Meijers Connie was well stocked with cleaning sponges that she would use as pads. (Kim prayed they didn't get mixed up with the kitchen sponges.) She got different colors for each day of the week. The theory went that instead of disposing of them, she would simply rinse and reuse. What about heavy nighttime flow? Just sleep naked and put a towel over the sheets.

Thank-God they had separate rooms, the sight of her naked bleeding roommate would have been too much for Kim to take. Strangely enough, the natural way is not always the easiest way. After several months Connie soon got tired of sponge wedgies and waking up looking like a pornographic horror star. So even though it went against the theory of vaginal empowerment, she succumbed and went crawling back to her good old friends Tampax and Maxi. Who knows, maybe one day tampons will be recycled…

Acid Reflux

College is a time of experimentation. People come out of their shells and are more open to fresh ideas and practices such as new diets or religion. Things that might have been perceived as elusive or taboo in the past might become alluring, like the forbidden fruit. This can be dangerous, as evil can sometimes disguise itself with innocence and mystery. As a college freshman,

Sally had been brought up in a strict Catholic household. Church every Sunday, grace before dinner, and prayers before bed each night.

Her parents were always stressing to her the importance of turning to God and staying away from the immorals of the world such as sex and drugs. Eager to continue her religious upbringing after high school, Sally chose a private Catholic college as her school of choice. Unfortunately, she soon learned that even the most spiritual of people can be chased by the devil.

One night after a hard week of prayer and study, Sally was at a social gathering and was offered acid. That's right: acid, LSD, tabs, trips, blotters, microdots. Maybe she thought it would bring her closer to God. But a short while after taking the pill Sally took off running out the door, down the stairs, outside, up the street, she took off like justice from the courts.

Good thing her two friends Adam and Eve went after her. They didn't want their poor delusional friend loose on the streets. "Sally stop! Come back! We love you! Don't leave us! Sall YYY!" But in her new state of mind Sally no longer saw them as Adam and Eve; they had transformed themselves into new beings: Adam was the devil, Eve was an angel. The closer they got to her, the faster she ran, screaming insanely: "Help! The devil is coming after me! Help Lord save me!" Two concerned friends are no match for a laced out chick with deviled delusions. She used her new energy to outrun them and disappear into the night. Lucky for Sally there was an angel looking out for her.

A homeless man who happened to be a Good Samaritan found her roaming through the park, and after some questioning managed to lead her back to her apartment. Sally's roommate Angelica was so grateful she gave him a half-eaten pizza and $5.00. After saying goodbye to her rescuer, Sally's trip was far from over. She certainly was in no mood for bed. "I saw the devil! I saw the devil! He was coming for me! He's coming for me!" Saint Angelica stayed up all night singing to her tripped out roomie, trying to ward off the acidic evils.

This was definitely not something that had been advertised in the college brochure. Fortunately, Sally chose to "Just Say No" after that crazed night. She learned that like crime, drugs just don't pay. Unless you happen to be a homeless man who rescues a tripped out chick in the park.

Can I Use Your Toothbrush?

In the teachings of Christianity, people are taught to share. Share with your family, share with your friends, share with your enemies, share with your sister's boyfriend's brother's neighbor's wife. This is all fine and dandy, as sharing usually is the moral thing to do most of the time. But with any good thing, there are always exceptions.

Gabby found this out the hard way during her senior year. She was a philosophy major who came to college armed with her bible, determined to change the world. Devoutly religious, she had been involved in one of the campus's Christian groups, The Cross Followers, since her freshmen year. So far, it had been a very enjoyable experience. She made lots of close friends with similar beliefs and it kept her away from such evil temptations as alcohol and sex.

Like many college groups, the Followers had their own place to call home. They rented two houses off campus where a select group of members were chosen to reside each year. Gabby had to wait three years to earn this honor, so she was ecstatic when she found out that she would be living in the womens' house for her senior year.

The Followers' houses each held twelve people, forced to share bathrooms and bedrooms. Despite the large amount of residents, the houses were pretty clean, especially the womens', as cleaning and cooking schedules were strictly enforced. For a reminder, a sign was kept up in the kitchen which read "Jesus washed others' feet, so you must wash your dishes!" Everything in the house was communal; food was always up for grabs. If a member asked you for something, it was considered selfish to refuse: "Can I finish your leftovers?" Answer: "Well, I was going to eat them for dinner tonight, but that's OK. I can cook something else instead. Help yourself." "If your enemies are hungry, feed them; if they are thirsty, give them a drink."- Proverbs 25:21

For the most part Gabby enjoyed living with her fellow Followers; it was nice being around people that looked out for each other. That all changed one fateful morning when Gabby forgot to set her alarm clock. She woke up in a panic, her class started in ten minutes. Rushing about the bathroom she noticed that her toothbrush was missing from the holder. With no time to spare, she quickly rinsed with Scope and scurried off to campus. When she returned later that day she discovered her toothbrush had mysteriously returned to its place. What was the deal here? Did an angel bring it back?

It turns out someone did bring back her toothbrush, but it wasn't an angel. When she mentioned it to her housemates that evening, one of them, Terrah, spoke up "Oh, that was me. I forgot to put it back last night." "What do you mean forgot to put it back?" Gabby asked suspiciously. Did she drop it in the toilet or something? "I threw out my toothbrush last week, so I've been using yours until I get a new one." Terrah answered matter-of-factly, as if it were a perfectly normal thing to just use someone's toothbrush.

For the first time in a long while, Gabby felt the rise of anger heat up in her. She was ready to blow her top and tell Terrah where she could bend over and take the toothbrush, but her fellow housemates were observing the scenario with interest. This could be seen as a "test of patience." Not wanting to lose her holy demeanor, Gabby took a deep breath and told Terrah that, in future, she would prefer it if she asked first before borrowing her toothbrush. "Do not share toothbrushes. Sharing a toothbrush could result in an exchange of body fluids and/or microorganism between the users of the toothbrush, placing the individuals involved at an increased risk for infections." -ADA

Gabby immediately went out and bought a new toothbrush, which she chose to store next to the bible for safe keeping. It just goes to show that even the righteous have their limits. Sure the bible has many stories of generosity and distribution, but nowhere does it say, "Thou shall share spit."

Bat Invasion

It's not uncommon for college students to live without air conditioning. While new dorms and apartments are usually equipped with this luxury, people living in older buildings aren't as lucky. That is why during the hot seasons many students feel like they're living in over-sized saunas. Scorching dwellings lead to an abundance of blowing fans and open windows, and as we all know, open windows can invite unwanted guests.

Fran and Tina had such an encounter during their senior year while living in an ancient sorority house. There were big old trees all around the property and at night bats would fly around the house. (Tough dilemma: would you rather sweat your ass off or sleep with a bat?)

One night the two girls were awakened by blood-curling screams. They got up to investigate and saw one of their housemates, Laurie, running up the stairs shrieking with an open umbrella above her head. It turns out that she had found a bat in her room and was a little frightened by this hairy intruder. Maybe it was because he hadn't bought her dinner first…

Laughing hysterically at their umbrella roomie, Fran and Tina decided to go back to bed, and this INFURIATED Laurie. Since Fran was the sorority house manager, Laurie screamed that it was, "her duty to get the bat out." But Fran told her that bats weren't in her job description so she was going back to bed. The girls retreated to their room crying with laughter, and Fran just happened to refer to Laurie as a "bitch" for wanting her to be a bat hunter.

The next second, Laurie was up the steps screaming in Fran's face that she, "WAS NOT A BITCH!" That was awkward. How'd she know? Laurie said she had heard them through the vent and didn't appreciate being referred to like that. Oops. Not exactly a bonding experience.

Somehow, the girls managed to survive the rest of night without getting rabies or vampire bites and the bat was dead the next morning after being hit with a tennis racket. Moral of the story: Never stand next to an open vent if you have to "vent."

If it Makes Penicillin, it Must Be Good!

Quite often in college, roommates are brought together by mutual friends, sort of like an arranged polygamous marriage. Suzy knows Suri, Suri knows Jane, Jane knows Joan, and this creates a recipe for a nine-month living utopia. After all, if Suzy and Suri are friends they're bound to get along, and if Jane likes Joan then Jane and Suzy should hit it off, and since Jane knows Joan then Joan should get along with everybody too, right?

WRONG! Mixing roommates can be a lot like working in a chemical lab. Sometimes the result will go well, but if you mix the wrong concoction you can have disastrous results. And a chemistry lab is safer than a college residence, because it is equipped with an emergency fire blanket and eyewash station. College students live unprotected and risk exposing themselves to toxic roommate waste.

Deanna had her own horrible roommate concoction during her sophomore year. She moved into an apartment with three other girls, and one of them, Tracy, was her best friend since high school. The other two, Karen and Becky, were Tracy's roommates from freshmen year. Deanna didn't really know them, but she knew Tracy really well and figured, "Well if Tracy likes them, I'm sure I will too." BIG MISTAKE.

You know the old saying that you don't really know someone until you live with them? That is why many roommates who begin as friends leave as enemies, because once they really know one another, they find out they can't stand each other! No wonder half of all marriages end in divorce, they learn too much about their spouse. That's why ignorance is bliss.

It turned that Deanna's best friend, Tracy, had the backbone of a jellyfish. Karen and Becky were both sloppy bitches, and the only reason she got along with them was because she let them walk all over her. Of course Deanna didn't know this when she signed the lease, and after that she was legally bonded into a living hell.

There was no honeymoon period for these four girls. Deanna started having doubts right after she moved in. At first it was the just the cleaning; Karen and Becky didn't believe in it. Initially Deanna tried the most common approach with this: A CLEANING SCHEDULE! Perfect idea right? Everything is divided up equally, with rotating weekly duties, and no one can argue because it is fair for all. Deanna made a typed, organized list and placed it proudly on the fridge for all to see. This is all fine and dandy if people are willing to abide by it, but time went by and Karen and Becky never lifted a finger. Soon their rooms smelled as if fungus was growing in there.

Deanna finally asked them why they weren't following the list, and they replied, "You didn't actually expect us to stick to that did you?" *Well yeah, dumb-asses, that was the whole point of making it!* She tried going to Tracy for help, but Tracy claimed the mess didn't bother her. The truth was she was just afraid to stand up to them.

At this point you might be thinking, "So what? A lot of people live with slobs," but it gets better. With no one on her side, Deanna then tried the "I'm not cleaning anymore" approach and hoped they would eventually do it themselves. Things went from dirty to a health hazard. The bathroom got worse and worse. Soon there was a huge, green mold ball next to the sink. Gross. Naturally, this disgusted Deanna beyond belief. She asked them why they didn't just clean the mold in the bathroom, and they said, "We want it there." If they had been apes, they probably would have been kicked out of the band...

Oh, and let's not forget about the dishes. Karen and Becky went beyond not washing them. Are you ready for this? They would use them, rinse them off (with no soap), and then put them back in the cupboard. Most of the dishes were covered with food crusts. Deanna started using plastic silverware because she couldn't trust anything in the cupboard. Here's the clincher:

these girls were blessed with a dishwasher, they just never bothered to use it. Maybe they were trying to create their own disease, who knows?

Deanna felt like her apartment should be quarantined. For her own health and sanity, she knew she had to get out of there. Thankfully, she found what is for some students a glimpse of heaven: A SUBLEASER! Karen's boyfriend, a knight in shining armor with missing teeth and BO, offered to take over her lease. She didn't hesitate; this was a way out! A few of her friends had an empty room to rent, and she moved in with them as soon as she could. Free at last, free at last, Thank God almighty, free at last! At least now she didn't have to worry about eating off of dirty dishes or mold growing near her toothbrush.

As for Tracy, it's no surprise that this whole ordeal put a mighty strain on their friendship. Ignore it and it will go away right? By not backing up her friend, she was siding with the bitches. Maybe a few more months of homegrown penicillin would help her grow a backbone, but in the meantime, she would have to eat the mold.

Weird Timing

After returning home from a vacation, it's customary to want to share your stories and experiences with friends and family. This is easily done with pictures, souvenirs, etc. Some vacation stories are better off being left on the trip, especially spring break memories. Ever seen "Girls Gone Wild?" Sometimes when young people travel to exotic places they end up coming back with more than just a sunburn.

Jamie saw this during her freshmen year. Right after spring break everyone was returning with fresh tan lines, new tattoos and piercings, and life-long memories. Of course they could probably only remember bits and pieces through the alcohol fog. When the cats are away the kids will play. You send a bunch of youths to Mexico where the drinking age is 18; and that's one tequila, two tequila, three tequila, floor.

Jamie's roommate, Sara, was one of the many college travelers that chose Mexico for her spring vacation. Jamie figured Sara would come back bursting with details about her drunken excursions, but she ended up being unusually quiet and withdrawn upon her return. Not a good sign.

No matter how much she was probed, Sara wouldn't tell anybody what was bothering her. Sometimes people just need the right moment to open up about their problems. One day Sara was on the phone with her mother and suddenly began screaming: "I don't know what to do Mom! I went to Cancun and I came back PREGNANT! What do I do! What do I do!" Everyone came out of their rooms to listen. Her secret was out.

Not exactly a tactful way to reveal a pregnancy. This was one souvenir Sara hadn't planned on getting. Hey, it could have been worse. At least she came back in one piece and didn't catch any diseases. That was certainly a trip Sara will never forget. She ended up leaving school and moving back home. With money tight and a baby to feed, let's hope she doesn't go on any more vacations for a LONG time.

Daddy Dearest

No matter how old a girl gets, whether or not she is fifteen or fifty, in the eyes of her father she is still always, "Daddy's little girl." A father sees it as his job to be the protector of the family, especially the females. And when a daughter starts dating, Daddy's safekeeping often goes into overdrive.

"Who are you going out with? We need to meet him first. Where are you going? What time will you be back? What do his parents do for a living? Does he have a criminal record?" Girls who experience this kind of overprotection often see college as an escape, but a lot of times this sheltering will follow them away from home.

Such was the case with Erin. Erin grew up in a very protective household. Her father was a strong man who worked for the prison system, and believed any male was a possible threat to his daughter. While growing up she was constantly reminded to lock doors, be aware of her surroundings, and never trust strangers.

Once she entered high school, any guy she wanted to go out with was first forced through a rigorous interrogation process. It was always a dreaded event for Erin and her dates. Alleluia! Time for college. True, her father could no longer stand over her shoulder, but he still went over basic rules whenever he talked to her. "Always keep your room locked at night. Never walk anywhere alone in the dark, and never accept a drink from a guy at a party. Who knows what he might slip into it!"

Even though it got annoying sometimes, Erin did appreciate her Dad's concern, and they kept a pretty good relationship. One day he came to campus to take her out to lunch and shopping. When they got back to the dorms he helped her carry the bags in, little did he know what he was about to encounter. It turns out that Erin's roommates were two idiots who always kept the door unlocked. They would tell people just to stop by and hang out even when they weren't home. Erin neglected to tell her Dad this, fearing his ugly reaction.

When Erin and Dad walked into the room, there were four guys relaxing on the couch. These poor boys picked the wrong time to come visit, because Daddy hit the roof. He thought they were there to rob or attack someone. "What the hell are you doing in here! Get out! I could have you all arrested! You'd better not come near my daughter again! Your asses will be thrown in jail!" Lucky for them he didn't pull out a gun.

Once the guys were scared away, Erin got a huge lecture about safety, after which he left and reminded her to lock the door. A few hours later her Mom called, telling her how unsafe that was and if Dad hadn't have come back to the room with her she could have been robbed, raped, murdered, etc. After that incident, Erin insisted that her roommates start locking the door when they leave. She didn't want another encounter of "father knows best." Perhaps this was a case of overreacting, but I'll tell you one thing, if more students took safety this seriously, it would definitely take a bite out of campus crime.

Computer Science

Of all the belongings of most college students, a computer tends to be one of the most useful and expensive possessions. Not only is it a source for typing papers, but it provides instant access for fun activities such as Internet surfing, E-mail, Facebook, and best of all: INSTANT MESSAGING. Want to chat with friends, strangers, or perverts? Just turn on the screen. I believe computers are the reason many students become hermits, they don't need people to socialize, they've got their keypads. Because of the great dependence on computers for academic and social needs, a student's life can be uprooted if their beloved toy has a malfunction.

Judy found this out during her senior year of college. She was living in an apartment off campus, and hoping her old computer would make it through one more year. Who wants to go to the computer lab when they can have it right in their room?

Once moved in Judy went out right away and bought a cord for the Internet connection, hooked it up, and anticipated sending out her first E-mails of the semester. Uh oh, something's not right. The connection wasn't working: no Internet, no E-mail, and NO INSTANT MESSAGING! What was a girl to do? Now Judy knew nothing about computers, so she didn't bother trying to figure it out herself. Luckily she had a friend, Carl, that she knew could help.

Carl was a computer science major, who better to ask for help with her problem? She called him up and pulled the old damsel in distress act, "Please help me Carl, my Internet isn't working and I don't know what to do!" Men love to come to a ladie's rescue.

Carl came over confidant he could fix the problem, but he too was stumped by the lack of Internet connection. He spent hours working on it, trying only what computer experts would understand, and still nothing worked. Fortunately Carl was not one to give up easily, especially since this was his specialty and he didn't want to lose face in front of a female.

He came back several more times to work on it, and Judy looked on hopefully as Carl experimented with different strategies on her computer. But he still was having no luck. She prayed he would somehow bring her computer back to life. After many frustrating hours, Carl was about to throw in the towel when he decided to do one last thing that he hadn't tried yet: check the connection.

Getting down on his knees he examined the cord attached to the wall and made a shocking discovery... "Judy... this is a phone cord," he said, smiling with humor and amazement. Bingo. Mystery solved. "Oh my God, I thought it was an Internet cord because it fit into the wall!" Judy answered with embarrassment and laughter. Too bad phone and Internet cords look alike.

To the unsuspecting computer illiterate, one could easily pass for the other.

"Well, I think we've found your problem. Just change the cord and you'll be all set", Carl said laughing. He also felt a little dumb, with all his knowledge that should have been the first thing he checked, a classic case of male arrogance.

Once Judy got a new cord plugged in, Internet came right back like an act of God, and she was grateful for all of Carl's active persistence. Judy's computer did have some spirit left, because it made it through the rest of the school year. As for Judy and Carl, they both went on to graduate with honors. Which proves that book smarts does not replace common sense. And they each learned a valuable lesson from this experience: before investing a huge amount of time and effort into solving a problem, first look for the simplest possible solution.

Nine-One What?

When people live together for a long time, conflict is practically unavoidable. As we have seen already from the stories in this book, sometimes roommates say and do things to each other that can lead to a Jerry Springer type brawl. But no matter how bad the friction becomes, it almost never leads to an emergency situation. Certainly nothing to warrant a

911 call…

Growing up we are taught that 911 is for, "emergencies only." Officers often visit schools and explain what does and doesn't require a 911 call. Children know better than to call it for something minor such as a skinned knee or a lost bike. But in the case of Angel and Linda, that lesson must have been forgotten after elementary school.

During their senior year of college these two shared a house off campus. They started out as good friends, but differing opinions on household cleaning caused their relationship to crumble. Basic problem: Angel cleaned, Linda didn't. Everything hit the roof one afternoon after Linda had failed once again to clean the bathroom. Words were exchanged, voices rose, and within seconds they were both screaming back and forth at each other. Linda threw a book in Angel's direction, and Angel retaliated by hurling a water bottle at her. Too bad there wasn't an RA around to resolve this.

"Watch me call 911!" Linda threatened. She picked up the phone, dialed, then hung up. She must have forgotten that 911 has caller ID, because the operator called right back and asked if everything was OK. Another roommate answered and explained that it was just a normal argument, but the operator was forced to send the police to investigate.

Within minutes an officer showed up at their door, wanting to know what led to the emergency call. Linda justified her actions because she said she felt threatened by the flying water bottle. Angel justified that Linda was a crazy bitch who wouldn't do her chores. God knows what was going through this cop's head. He asked how old they were. "Twenty-two? Well then act like it. Next time I could take you both in for domestic abuse."

Then he left and the tension remained. At least the cop did his part to protect the peace. No more 911 calls were made from their house that year. Maybe they learned a lesson about mature phone use, but their house did end up getting banned from pizza delivery for the rest of the semester. It's not a good idea to swear at the pizza place when you're hungry. Case in point: be wary when you use the phone. It could end up getting you arrested; or worse yet, banned from pizza service.

Bible Time

Contrary to popular belief, college is not just a place where kids can party while working towards a degree. It is also a time of self-exploration and growth, a transition period from high school to adulthood, and for some people, an era to find God. It's amazing how many people enter college being somewhat religious and end up coming out able to recite half the bible. Which; I might add, is much healthier than learning how to bong a beer.

Thanks to the abundance of various religious groups offered on campus, it is easy for students to find a place to worship. They often find such joy and solace with their beliefs that they want to share them with others, and in some cases help save their souls. But as we all know, not everyone wants to be saved...

Cindy had such an experience during her junior year. Her roommate, Brenda, was very involved in one of the campus bible studies. She would spend hours reading the bible and highlighting passages, and she would always try to get Cindy to join her. Cindy's response?

"Hey, I say my prayers at night and I already do enough reading for class."

Cindy didn't mind her roommate's bible dedication, but she did mind Brenda's attempts to bring her salvation. Whenever Cindy would be getting ready to go out partying, Brenda would read passages of the bible out-loud to her. "Blessed is the man who endureth temptation: for when he is tried, he shall receive the crown of life." (New Testament, James, Chapter 1, verse 12.) "Cindy, the devil is tempting you with the evils of the world, you need to resist him!"

Did Brenda forget that Jesus turned water into wine? As they say, you can't save everybody. Brenda failed at her attempt to pull Cindy from the devil's grip, because Cindy continued to go out to parties the rest of the year.

Let's just hope mercy is placed on her soul.

Rude Awakening

For most college students, early morning classes are avoided like the plague. Because college life is filled with so much late nighttime activity (bars, video games, studying, movies, or just staying up discussing the meaning of life) the last thing one wants to do is get up for anything that starts before noon. And even worse than that is when you don't need to wake up early, but are drafted into it because of roommate distractions.

Now it's normal to get your sleep disturbed when sharing a bedroom: waking up and going to sleep at different times, opening and closing doors, rummaging for things in the dark. Because people have different schedules, alarms go off and inadvertently wake up two instead of one. These things are acceptable because most of the time they can't be avoided. Once you are out of the dorms and have your own room, you don't have to deal with those kinds of distractions right?

But some people seem to assume that because a person is sleeping, they are also temporarily deaf. Bridgett discovered this the hard way during her sophomore year. She shared an apartment with two other girls, Chris and

Laura, and didn't like either one of them. Of course they had appeared to be nice and normal when they all signed the lease. Lease signing often has a Dr. Jekyll and Mr. Hyde reaction for people; where Jekyll turns to Hyde once the deal is made.

Bridgett would have been content just keeping to herself and ignoring them, but her ears would not allow it. Her roommates were notorious for playing music in the morning, putting it on full blast while they sang in the shower or dried their hair.

Bridgett put up with these morning concerts for an amazingly long time. She tried earplugs, and then tried holding a pillow over her head. She wanted to just break their radio, but she was trying to avoid a big blowout at all costs. Bridgett tried asking them politely to keep the music down in the morning, but it fell on deaf ears. Have you heard the saying, "You can't have peace without war first?" Well in some situations this is true…

One morning brought Bridgett to her breaking point. She was sound asleep and in the middle of a great dream involving Brad Pitt, when Madonna's, "Papa Don't Preach," song jerked her awake. That's it, when you mess with a woman's elite sexual dreams you are bound to see wrath. Throwing back the covers, she stormed out of her room and screamed, "Turn your fucking music off! I can't fucking sleep!" Chris's response…brace yourself...

"Well maybe if you would've asked me nicer, I would have turned it down the first time." What in God's name was this girl's definition of "nice?" A formal letter begging her to let others sleep? In the end Bridgett's explosive outburst put a stop to the morning music. When the peaceful method didn't work, she resigned to a good old-fashioned cuss-out, making sure her voice was louder than Madonna's. Bridgett still didn't like her roommates, but at least now she could sleep and fantasize in peace.

Auto Repair

Although this story is not gross or frightening; it's a life lesson everyone should have before adulthood. A classic example of the old saying, "ADMIT TO NOTHING". At various points in life, everyone is bound to have some type of car trouble. Flat tire, run out of gas, accident, breakdown, etc. This is usually a huge inconvenience because it affects your time, transportation, and often puts a big hole in your wallet. A car is a lot like a human body, it can be very unpredictable. Sometimes things go wrong without any warning, and the source of the problem is not always found.

Carlton had such car trouble during his senior year of college. One morning he was about to leave for class, but found he had a slight problem:

the reverse was out on his beloved seven year- old truck. Just like that, gone. It wouldn't budge backward. What a great way to start the day. But Carlton was resourceful, and he shifted to neutral and managed to push it out the driveway.

Not a smart idea to drive around without reverse, but he dreaded the repair cost. So he put off taking it in and continued backing his truck in neutral. This process of neutral pushing went on for several weeks until he finally brought it in to be repaired. Problem solved? It's never that simple in this book.

The shop soon called him up with some bad news, "Sorry sir, we couldn't find the source of your reverse issue." Translation: "Sorry sir, you're screwed." Hard to fix a car if you don't know what's wrong with it. What was a guy to do? Fortunately for Carlton, he had a job, and generous parents. They told him that if he could find a car for under $300 a month, they would pay for half.

Pretty good timing, because a local dealership was having a 3-year lease special for $250 a month. And get this...they agreed to take his truck as a trade in! When they asked whether it had any problems, Carlton replied, "Let's just say it's been around the block" Hey, at least he was being honest. Fingers crossed, he watched as they drove it around the lot for appraisal.

Right turn, left turn, a few circles... It was definitely his lucky day, because they never once put it in reverse. NOT ONCE. There was no negotiating the $2200 that was offered for it. Not a bad deal for a truck that needed manual pushing. Carlton was elated with this sweet outcome.

Any trace of a guilty conscience? Naw. Carlton had no problem justifying his trade-in. The way he saw it, people get screwed over so much with cars; it's time the dealer had a turn. With the help of his wits and the generosity of a naive dealership, finally a poor college student managed to get the better end of a sale. Once the papers were signed, there was no going back. As he drove off in his new car, Carlton grinned as he saw his old truck being priced to sell. Suckers. Still no guilt, but he hoped whoever wanted to buy it would first try to back it up.

Bare Necessities

Before moving in with new roommates, it's customary to get in touch with each other to determine who's bringing what. This saves a lot of inconvenience on move in day so there aren't multiple refrigerators, couches, etc. With the lack of space in the dorms there just isn't enough room for extra amenities. If everyone brings some necessity, it keeps things fair and livable. But in some cases, people just aren't willing to do their share.

Deb found this out firsthand right before her freshmen year. She didn't know any of her three future roommates, but she was excited to meet and get to know them. At the end of the summer she called up each girl to introduce herself and discuss what they were going to bring. She told them she already had a fridge, microwave, and rug that she could contribute. When she asked them what they were bringing the main response was: "toothpaste."

Needless to say, these four girls did not start out on the right roommate foot. Deb was the only one who bothered to bring anything for the room. No one brought any furniture; there was no place to sit except the bunk beds. Can you imagine? Deb finally broke down and bought a cheap TV and she borrowed an old VCR from home. No one bothered to thank her for making their room livable. Maybe they had just got out of prison and were used to surviving with the bare minimum. Besides the lack of room contribution, these girls also had no problem eating all of Deb's food.

When she would confront them about it, they would always say it wasn't them. Well it certainly couldn't be any of their friends; they only socialized with each other, preferring the solitude of their dorm. And they were in bed every day by 10:00 PM; even on the weekends!

After one semester of living with these thieving mooches, Deb had had enough and moved out, taking all of her appliances with her. They were left with no TV, fridge, or microwave. That was the best revenge she could have given, a classic taste of your own medicine. Let's hope these three found another way to feed themselves, or else they'd probably started rummaging through the trash outside. Hey, it's cheaper than ordering pizza.

False Threats

When you live in an apartment, paying rent is a fact of life. No one wants to do it, but they must if they want to keep a roof over their heads. Money problems are a common woe for most college students, which can lead to some heated disputes over bill payments. Sometimes these quarrels get real ugly; as certain people think their bills are everyone's responsibility but their own. Desperate times call for desperate measures, and it's amazing what people will do to get out of paying their debts.

Dora had such an encounter during her sophomore year. She lived in an apartment with four other girls, and halfway through the year one of them, Cammie, decided to stop paying rent. Just like that, no more payments. She didn't mention anything to her roommates, so it was quite a shock when the landlord called seeking the money. Of course they confronted her about it, and she assured them that she would take care of it.

Remember the old saying: "Money talks and bullshit walks?" Be prepared, you'll hear a lot of bullshit in life. The only thing Cammie seemed to be interested in was sleeping with her boyfriend. He was over every night, and the sound of the bed squeaking could always be heard: "Yeah baby! Right there! Give it to me! Yeah! Show me the money!"

Too bad she never showed the landlord any money. Another month went by along with one more missed payment. This time Deb and the others were furious with her. She had lied to them! This led to a huge blowout and ended with Cammie saying she had had enough and was going back home. She moved out that same day.

Once home, she called the landlord and explained that she left because her roommates had threatened her with a knife. Not true. All they had threatened her with was a lawsuit, which is actually scarier than a knife. Fortunately the landlord didn't buy her demented story of knife-wielding roommates. *Word of caution*: you lose credibility when you owe someone money.

A few weeks later the girls found out the real reason Cammie picked up and left. It turns out that all of those nights of passion led to an unexpected pregnancy; this proved she wasn't spending her rent money on birth control. Do you think Dora and the others let her off the hook? Hell no! They took her to court and she ended up paying all she owed. Thank God for our wonderful judiciary system. It just goes to show that if someone won't cough up the dough, when all else fails, sue their ass, pregnant or not.

Peanut Butter Killer

Allergies are a very common annoyance for many people. There is such a broad range of allergies that one can be allergic to anything and everything from plants, animals, dust, clothes, and of course: food. This can put a real damper on what someone is able to eat and encounter. *Too bad more Americans aren't allergic to super-sized meal portions, or else our obesity epidemic would go way down.*

Taylor had endured peanut allergies her entire life. Not only could she not consume them, but just being around the little buggers could trigger an unpleasant reaction such as nausea, hives, and swelling. In elementary school, this condition allowed her to be in the "peanut free" classes, safe havens for the school's vulnerable nut victims.

Once in college she had to fend for herself against this tiny enemy. True it was an annoyance, but when the time came to leave home she had become accustomed to her nut-free life. *Men not included.* Little did she know that one twisted roommate would exploit this weakness against her like kryptonite to Superman.

From the start of the semester Taylor and her roommate, Molly, did not get along. Another friendship gone sour by cohabitation. They were sorority sisters who had decided to get an apartment together, and right away there were warlike confrontations over some very serious issues:

Molly: "Why'd you take my sweater!"

Taylor: "I swear bitch I never wore your fucking sweater!"

Molly: "Well then why is it all stretched out? Only your fat ass could do this!"

Like the old saying goes, you don't truly know someone until you live with them. Our country would probably have a lower divorce rate if couples lived separately.

One day Taylor came back from class and found a deadly intruder sitting on the coffee table. He was short, round, topless, with the name *Jif* spelled across him. He appeared to be friendly and appetizing, but Taylor wasn't fooled by his innocent appearance. She stayed back out of the line of fire and called a neighbor over to dispose of this uninvited peanut butter guest.

Molly's excuse for this unwanted intruder? She was running late for class and forgot to clean up after lunch. Nice try honey. She would have been better off saying the peanut fairy paid them a visit. Taylor hoped this was just an isolated incident, but no such luck. A week later she found a half-eaten peanut butter and jelly wedged into the couch, and then a few peanut M&M's somehow made their way into the bathroom. What the heck? Did this freak eat while she shit? Taylor was terrified that her food would be tampered with next. She could see the paper headlines: College Student Dies: Death by Nut.

What was a girl to do? Fortunately peer pressure can be more intimidating then a prison term. When word got out about Molly's demented tactics, their sorority friends threatened to revoke her membership unless she went nut-free. Despite the fact that she was trying to kill one of her fellow sisters, there was no way Molly wanted to leave this loving sisterhood. She promised to be more careful about deadly intruders in the apartment. As for Taylor, she managed to survive the rest of the school year without any severe allergic reactions. But she kept her eyes open and was always on guard for another Jif invader.

Secret Fetish

There are many honorable jobs on a college campus, many of which are held by poor students struggling to buy their next beer or book. From the RA's who settle squabbles to the cafeteria workers who help make the food appear edible, students have plenty of opportunities to earn their keep. One position, however, stands above all the rest. Can you guess what it is? These workers monitor who enters the buildings 24-7, they watch drunks stumble in at 4 AM, oversee the phones, and most important. ..SORT THE MAIL! Hold your applause, this job is a Dorm Deskie!

Deskies are the ones who man the front desk at each residence hall. They are a dorm's first line of defense. Friendly deskies help a dorm appear welcoming and pleasant, greeting those who pass by. Unlike most campus jobs, they rarely deal with bodily fluids, and it allows students the chance to get out of their rooms, sit on their butts, and get paid. So it is often a much-sought out position.

Trish was a sophomore and a second-year deskie. She enjoyed watching people come and go, using work time to study, and reading magazines that were ordered through the mail. Overall her job was pretty uneventful, until one girl's mail order items came up missing. Was it letters from home, money, food, or medicine?

No, those are all things you can live without. It turns out this girl was on a lingerie kick and had ordered some nighties from a catalog. She anxiously awaited her new items, but they never arrived. Suspicions rose around the deskies who sorted the mail, and soon Trish became the prime suspect.

Now Trish knew she had borrowed the occasional Cosmo that came in, but she was no panty thief! Besides, she and the victim weren't exactly the same size. Poor Trish, not only was she accused of being a thief, she was also accused of being fat! Trish was a tiny thing that hovered around 100 pounds, and her accuser was at least a deuce and a half. Maybe she thought lingerie would make her folds seem sexy?

Now if Trish was going to steal clothes, wouldn't she take something that fit? No one else seemed to believe this logic. While Trish proclaimed her innocence, the local police were soon involved. They contacted Trish and told her that her room would be getting searched soon for missing items. This was a classic example of police brilliance. You think someone is hiding stolen goods, so you warn them ahead of time that you are coming to search their property. In case Trish was hiding anything, she certainly had enough time to get rid of it.

The SWAT Team soon arrived at Trish's dorm pounding on the door in full body armor with guns drawn. (Not really, it was only two pimple-faced cops who couldn't find a job anywhere else.) Trish watched helplessly as her belongings were scrutinized. Was that cop smelling her underwear?

After a thorough search of bras, panties, shirts, skirts, and sheets, no contraband was found. The cops walked away empty-handed, hanging their heads in shame. After all, a bust like that could have boosted their careers. As for Trish, she continued on with her deskie career that year. No longer a theft suspect, she just hoped the real thief would one day be brought to panty

justice.

That's Not a Toilet!

Potty training is one of the first milestones children face. It marks graduation from infancy to toddlerhood. It's a huge step because they are learning to control their bodily functions and understand the concept of toilet usage. In most circumstances, a child can't even enter kindergarten until they are capable of wiping their own ass. By the time they enroll in college, most students have been potty-trained at least 15 years, but that doesn't mean that they can't have a relapse. With the help of alcohol, many college students are able to regress back to their pre- toilet trained days, leaving urine and excrement in the oddest of places. Hopefully, once they enter the real world most students have outgrown this habit of toilet avoidance. That is why I believe that toilet training does not end once a person is out of diapers, but after college.

Fridge Washer

Late-night snacks are a common occurrence in college. Students get accustomed to staying up late studying, drinking, gaming, etc. Once 2AM rolls around the stomach starts to get restless for some solid food; so a food break is usually needed. This is especially true once the bars close, nothing like a few beers to bring on the cravings. Too late to call for a pizza delivery? Just hope the fridge has some leftovers in it.

Fridges are a great resource for college students. Unlike most apartment furnishings, a fridge is quite durable towards young, drunken stupidity. It's tall (can't be sat on or slept on), heavy (not easily moved), and durable. One would think that since it's built so solid, not much could happen to a fridge in a room full of drunks. But as this book always proves, never doubt the power of inebriation.

Rocky discovered this fact during his junior year. While playing cards at a friend's apartment, he had a few too many and then passed out on the couch. His friends played on, drinking beer into the wee hours of the morning while Rocky snored away. After a while he woke up and stumbled towards the fridge, peering intently into the contents inside. His friends assumed he was looking for food and ignored him, BIG MISTAKE.

To everyone's horror, Rocky suddenly unzipped his pants and started pissing into the fridge. That's right, wizzing away. His drunken urination was quickly stopped as they pulled him away, but the damage was done. It seems that since the fridge was hard and white, Rocky had mistaken it for a urinal.

Needless to say, all of the contents inside had to be thrown out. At least he was caught in the act, if it had gone unnoticed some poor saps might have ended up eating pissed food. Let's hope Rocky cut back on the drinking, or else he would mark his territory on other innocent appliances.

Turd Burglar

As young adults living away from home, college students often rely on their roommates to help them out in little ways: a ride to the store, taking phone messages, waking them up for class, holding their hair back when they puke, etc. Roommates often become a sort of surrogate second family, and it's nice knowing you have people you can rely on when you need help. There are some things, however, that go way beyond everyday living assistance.

Amber, Danielle, and Kristen were all seniors living in an apartment off-campus. One night after a major drinking binge, Kristen was kicked out of the bar and ended up sleeping at a neighboring guys' apartment. After praying to the Porcelain God for a while, she ended up passed out on their couch.

The next morning when Amber left to go to the football game she ran into Kristen as she came walking back to their apartment. The best way to describe Kristen was: "She looked like she got ran over by a truck." Mascara was smeared under her eyes, her hair messed up, and there was vomit all over her shirt. "What happened to you?" Amber asked, shocked at her roommate's slovenly appearance. Kristen simply mumbled, "I don't know," and kept walking back.

It wasn't until that night that Amber got the full scoop of what had transpired. The neighbor guys invited her over and when she got there they were all laughing and grinning like they were the keepers of a hilarious secret. "Did you hear what Kristen did last night?" one of them asked with a devilish smile. "No, she wouldn't tell me, but she looked like hell when I saw her this morning," Amber replied, her curiosity now at its peak. She was also starting to feel a little concerned: bad things can happen when drunken girls are left to pass out in a guys' apartment…

What she learned next filled her with both relief and disgust. It turned out that in her drunken stupor Kristen mistook a chair for a toilet and left a big turd on it. One of the guys found it in the middle of the night and called her other roommate, Danielle, to come and clean it up. Amber couldn't believe it: Danielle actually got up in the middle of the night and walked down to that apartment to clean up her roommate's shit! All the while Kristen was passed out on the floor.

It gets better. After Danielle cleaned up the chair, put a blanket over Kristen and went back up to bed, her phone rang again a few hours later. The guys had found *another one* of Kristen's "presents" that morning under a rug in the living room. Not knowing what else to do, Danielle slipped on her latex gloves and went back down to clean up her roommate's excrement. They sure don't put that in the college brochures.

Kristen spent the rest of day sleeping off her hangover and shame. Her roommates were nice enough not to tease her about her blacked out shitting experience, but the guys weren't so tactful. They took pictures of it and told everyone that one of their neighbors had crapped all over their apartment. They started calling her the "Turd Burglar." Needless to say, Kristen was pretty embarrassed, but there is a lesson to be learned from this: better safe than sorry, after you go out drinking, put on a diaper before bed.

Bed Wetter

Nocturnal enuresis, or more commonly known as bed-wetting, is a typical part of growing up. Even once a child is fully potty-trained; it can be very easy to have an occasional nightly accident. So in case you happened to be a child bed-wetter, don't worry, you aren't alone. The body just doesn't always wake-up to announce that the bladder is full. The result: wet pajamas and a changing of the sheets. Most kids will grow out of this problem on their own, but as we know by now, college students have a tendency to regress.

Too much alcohol consumption can force someone back into infant-like conduct. They cry freely, have trouble walking, talking, and worst of all: bladder control. It's very easy to pass out and wet the bed after a night of liver damage. What could be worse than peeing in your own bed? Soaking up someone else's.

This is exactly what happened to Allan during his sophomore year. One night he and his roommates didn't have anything better to do, so they decided to have a contest and see who could drink the most alcohol in one hour. *Word of caution: Don't try this unless you want to end up dead or getting your stomach pumped.*

After five beers and four shots, Allan was declared the winner. Surprisingly there was no trophy. He decided to celebrate by walking over to his girlfriend's dorm to get laid and afterwards ended up passing out in her bed. In the middle of the night she woke up to find that everything: her bed, sheets, clothes, and hair, were wet. Thinking it was just sweat from their wild fornication, she ignored it and went back to sleep.

The next morning Allan was awakened by a soaked sensation between his legs. Knowing it was too much to be caused by a wet dream; he glanced down and saw that he had pissed out about half a gallon of urine onto the bed. This forced him to alert his girlfriend, putting an end to their blissful morning.

She was literally ...pissed! Anyone would be unless they were into golden showers. "You asshole! You pissed all over my bed! Well you'd better go exchange it with yours! I'm sure as hell not sleeping on that anymore!" With his pants still marinated with pee, Allan carried her damp, smelly mattress to his room, and then brought his dry mattress back to replace hers. Fortunately for him, his girlfriend had a very forgiving nature.

That was the last time Allan ever took part in a drinking contest. Smart thinking, because he didn't have any more beds to give away. And from then on whenever he went to sleep drunk he always made sure to pee beforehand, just like his Mom used to always remind him to. "Honey, don't forget to use the potty before going nighty night." Some rules are timeless.

Not in the Shower!

Like most transfer students, Wanda began her new college experience living in the dorms, despite the fact that she was already a junior and most upper classmen had moved off campus. The dorms offer new students a chance to meet lots of people, and Wanda was hoping to have nice roommates that would show her the ropes and help her adjust to campus life. Little did she know, she was about to be placed with a girl who had a habit so odd and disturbing that it must never be discussed at meal time.

Wanda had three roommates, and got along well with two of them, Stacey and Ali. While they weren't best friends, the three of them lived peacefully together in the small, cramped space they were provided. Their fourth roommate, Libby, was a different story. Libby was the quiet type, who kept to herself and rarely left the room except to eat or go to class. She definitely didn't have much of a social life, and perhaps this was why she didn't bother to keep herself clean. She only showered about twice a week, her blond hair was greasy and stringy, and she wore baggy sweatsuits and shuffled around in Minnie Mouse slippers. Her teeth were yellow and looked like they hadn't been brushed in years.

Despite these annoyances, Wanda and the others made the best of the situation and tried to ignore Libby's odor and hermit-like lifestyle. They soon realized, however, that there was something about Libby that was impossible to ignore…

One day while cleaning the bathroom, Wanda had a discovery in the shower that made her stomach churn and the blood drain from her face. Lying inside the drain was a piece of human feces. That's right: feces, dung, excrement, poop, crap, and most famously known as: shit. "Oh my God, you guys get in here and see this!" Wanda screamed. Once everyone got over their initial shock, they determined that Libby must be the culprit. No care-fronting in this situation, this called for a total bitch attack.

As soon as Libby got back from class, Wanda stormed up to her: "Did you crap in the shower?" Libby immediately lowered her head and stared at the floor, like a small child caught in a lie. "Answer me! Did you crap in the shower?" Slowly Libby raised her head up and mumbled, "I only did it once...I'm sorry..." "Sorry? Sorry? Libby that is disgusting! We were showering with your shit!" Wanda wheeled around and stormed out of the room, she had to get out of there before she completely lost it and threw Libby out the window, or worse, into the shower.

Later on that day the girls went to see their RA, Sara, all looking a little green in the face. "We've got something to tell you ..."they began, in a tone that made Sara think: "Oh great, I should've locked the door..." "You're kidding, right?" Sara asked after she heard about Wanda's gruesome discovery. By the looks of their faces, it was obvious this was no joke. Certainly not an issue that had been covered in RA training. "I'll have to talk to Scott about this." Scott was the dorm director; he was the one the RA's went to when there was a major problem like shit in the drain.

A meeting was soon called between Libby, Sara, and Scott. They first addressed the hygiene issue, with Sara telling Libby that she had to shower at least every other day; and *everyday* when she was on her period. Maybe she thought the odor would attract guys, like how female animals in heat lure mates with their scent.

As the meeting wound down, Scott saved the best for last: "And of course Libby, we can't have fecal matter in the shower." Fecal matter? That wasn't good enough for Sara. Libby might think that "fecal matter" was soap! "What Scott means is; you cannot poop in the shower." Sara couldn't believe her own voice. Did she really have to tell someone this? Libby seemed to be in full compliance. "OK, OK," she answered while nervously nodding her head.

The meeting ended and both Sara and Scott sighed with relief, praying they wouldn't have to address the issue again. Fortunately for Wanda and the others, Libby kept half the deal and no longer used the shower as a toilet. Her hygiene didn't really improve, but that could be overlooked as long as they weren't showering with her excrement.

"Because I Can!"

When you have overnight guests, it is a good idea to be prepared in order to be a gracious host. Have a place for them to sleep, enough food to share, and activities to keep everyone busy. Graciousness is usually not a top priority for college students, but since space and food are often limited; planning for guests is usually a smart idea.

Having guests brings additional responsibility because you are not only responsible for your own actions, but also those of whomever you bring into your habitat. For example: Johnny's buddy, Tom, comes to visit one weekend. One night in a drunken stupor, Tom accidentally breaks Johnny's roommate; Bob's, stereo. Tom goes home the next day, Bob has no idea how to contact him. Who do you think Bob is going to come after to pay for his stereo? That's right: It's your lucky day Johnny! Next time let Tom stay at home and you go visit.

No doubt about it, things can happen when there are extra people put into the mix, especially in a small space such as a dorm. It's like rats in a cage; get too many in there and they turn into cannibals. So if you're real fortunate your visitors will come and go without incident. And with a little luck, nothing will happen that will require monetary pay back.

Jerry had an interesting experience when his buddy, Doug, came to visit one weekend. Their schools had a rival football game against each other that Saturday, so it was a good time to get together. Since they hadn't seen each other in a while, the guys made up for lost time by drinking away most of the day. Tailgating, going to the bar after the game, and then hitting a party at night. Needless to say both guys were pretty tanked by the time they got back to Jerry's dorm in the wee hours of the morning.

The floor rocking beneath their feet, they stumbled in and crashed within minutes. Jerry couldn't make it into his bunk, so he passed out in the armchair, and Doug curled up on the couch. A few hours later, Jerry was awakened by the light from the hallway shining in his room. He realized that the door was wide open and Doug was off the couch. "What the hell is he doing?" Jerry muttered as he hauled himself up.

He was not prepared for what he saw next. Standing right outside the door was Doug, pissing on the wall with his pants around his ankles. Thank God no one else came into the hallway, who knows what they would have thought seeing Doug with his pants down and Jerry standing there watching. "Dude, what the hell are you doing? Why are you pissing in the hallway?" Doug's drunken response was one of wisdom and clarity. "Because I can!" He answered with a tipsy smile.

Jerry pulled him back into the room and left the piss to dry. No one ever cleaned it, so Doug left his permanent marking on the campus. If you ever wonder why some dorms smell, there is likely old piss seeped into the carpet. Jerry never told anyone in the dorm what happened, word spreads fast and if the wrong people found out he would likely have to pay a cleaning fee or some shit like that. A word of advice: sometimes the best way to save your ass is to keep your mouth shut. One of the good things about living around a lot of people is it's real easy to blame others for stuff.

Jerry got pretty lucky in this situation. There were plenty of nice toys in the room that Doug could have chosen as his toilet (TV, Game Cube, stereo, I-pod). At least this incident gave the guys a funny story to tell their friends back home. But the next time Doug came to visit, Jerry insisted he pee before bed.

"Is That What I Think it is?"

There is a prevalent philosophy in college life: work hard, party harder. After an evening of heavy partying, it is not uncommon to finish off the night with some spiritual enlightenment, such as praying to the Porcelain God. A toilet can be a great friend to a drunk because it will hold you up while you puke and listen to your tales of woe without criticism, unless you get a toilet that backs up. Often if one hears their roommate vomiting from drunken sickness, it is a common courtesy to check on them to make sure they aren't going to pass out and drown.

By her senior year in college Sandy was a veteran student and used to being both the drunken patient and the caregiver. She was living in an apartment with four other girls, and one night one of her roommates, Erin, came back from the bar after having one too many. The retched sounds of sickness in the bathroom forced Sandy to knock and ask if she was all right. "Yeah, I'll be fine," Erin said between barfs. Since Erin was coherent enough to talk, Sandy let her be. A few minutes later she heard the toilet flush and Erin stumbled to her room. "I'm sure she feels better now," Sandy thought with a grin. Little did she know that Erin had left a little surprise for her...

The next morning when Sandy entered the bathroom, she was stunned by what she saw. On the rug, toilet roll, mirror, and counter were dark brown smears. It looked like mud, too bad that wasn't the case. "Is that what I think it is? Oh, gross! What else could it be? Sick!" Apparently Erin had had a case of the beer shits the night before and didn't get it all in the toilet. How it got spread all over everything no one knows: it was one of those situations where it's better to don't ask or tell. *See no evil, hear no evil, speak no evil.*

Now Sandy was a nice and patient person, maybe even *too* nice sometimes. Instead of dragging Erin out of bed to clean up her own shit, Sandy got out the disinfectant and cleaned up. All the while she made a lot of noise by bitching, "This is so damn gross! I can't believe I am doing this!"

Her outbursts got the attention of her other roommates, and soon they were all crowding around and were both appalled and amused by what had happened. Since girls usually can't keep secrets, in a few hours all of their friends knew about Erin's bathroom disaster. For days afterwards people were coming up to Sandy and saying, "So, I hear Erin left you a nice mess to clean." At least it gave Sandy a good story to tell.

As for Erin, she was pretty embarrassed when she woke up and found out what had happened. Apparently she had no idea she had missed the toilet and smeared shit all over. Maybe she thought it was finger paint? "I am so sorry, I didn't know," she said with surprise and shame. "You could have woken me up to clean it! You're not going to tell anyone are you?"

Too late. Naturally Erin didn't want anyone to find out, but that was too much to hope for. Lucky for her, stories die fast and soon people had other things to talk about. And wouldn't you know it; that was the last time she ever left shit outside the toilet. Sometimes a little embarrassment goes a long way.

Reeked Revenge

When a college student leaves their bodily fluids in inappropriate places, it is often the result of craziness, stupidity, or drunkenness. The culprit is generally embarrassed when their behavior is brought to attention, and this usually ends the problem. However, there are rare occasions where one might do this leakage intentionally for their own twisted agenda.

This is exactly what happened freshmen year when Greg, Mike, Nate, and Jim lived together their first semester in the dorms. They had all moved in not knowing any of their new roommates, and for the most part it worked out well. Greg, Mike, and Nate all hit it off right away and were soon hanging out together all the time. They would stay up till 5: OO AM playing video games, and often stumble in together on the weekend nights. It was male bonding at its best, but not everyone approved.

Their fun freshmen experience was a real annoyance for Jim. It turned out that Jim was one of the few people who came to college not wanting any type of a social life. He hated sharing his space and would only speak when spoken to. At first the other guys tried to get him to come out of his shell and socialize, but he never wanted to. Some people like staying isolated. He rarely left the room except to eat and go to class. On weekends he spent his nights watching TV and playing on the Internet.

As the semester went on Jim's attitude went from cold and distant to outright hostility. He started complaining about little things such as the TV being left on (they didn't pay for electricity) or the guys being too loud while he was chatting online. God forbid if a pizza box was left out, one time they forgot to get rid of one and the next day found it taped to the door with a note, "Take out your pizza boxes you lazy dicks!" That was the last straw; the guys no longer bothered trying to get along with Jim. They decided to let him be a jerk and they would just ignore him.

Good news came towards the end of the semester; Jim announced that he was moving to another dorm because he couldn't stand living there anymore. Good-riddance buddy. That first night without Jim was one big party as they drank beer and stayed up swapping Jim stories. Little did they know that Jim had left them something to remember him by...

There was only one iron in the room, shared for occasional use. They soon noticed that something was different about the iron though, because it began leaving their clothes reeking afterwards. Finally Greg opened it up to see what was wrong and made a wretched discovery: the liquid inside it was not water, but urine. That's right: urine, piss, wizz, pee, whatever you want to call it. It turns out Jim found a place to leave his mark before moving out.

Needless to say, the guys were pissed! No pun intended. And they began brainstorming ways to get even with Jim. Go to his new room and piss on the bed? Put up degrading fliers around campus? But they never had a chance to follow through with anything, because after one week in his new dorm Jim moved back home. Newsflash: if you hate sharing space and being around people, a dorm is not a good place for you. At least the guys were able to live out the rest of the year in peace, after buying a new iron.

MAN'S BEST

FRIEND...THE CAT

Whoever said the dog is man's best friend probably never went away to college. Cats are a much more common pet for the college student because they are simple to care for and easy to hide from detection. Landlords won't ever hear a barking cat. The love for one's pet can drive people to extreme measures and in some cases illegal acts. The following stories are examples of how some students challenged authority regarding their beloved pussies. Some escaped from the jaws of rules and policy, others weren't so lucky.

Saving Money

It's not uncommon for students to have problems when renting a place to live. Most are inexperienced and have never rented before and this makes them easy prey for greedy landlords. When signing a lease, they either don't read the fine print or don't bother to follow it. This can put them in a type of "you're screwed" situation if they have problems with their living arrangements. For example: your roommate left, so it's your responsibility to pay their rent or take them to court. Moving out because you're graduating early? Congratulations: either find a subleaser or foot the bill.

Renting problems are usually all about saving money or breaking the rules, which is why many students try sneaking in extra roommates or pets that they aren't supposed to have. Your apartment doesn't allow cats, but you couldn't stand to leave your kitty at home? Sorry, that's a $600 fine to be shared between you and your roommates.

While many places do allow pets, there is always a price, usually either one big payment or a monthly fee. Who wants to pay an extra $30 a month for a pet? That's as much as cable! This is why many students get in trouble when it comes to pets and their wallets pay the price. Some students, however, are able to dodge the bullet of pet fees and live happily with their animals. They are either lucky enough not to get caught or are somehow able to outsmart the system.

Clay had such an experience during his junior year. He and his roommate Jimmy shared an apartment along with their cat, Fluffy. Like a lot of pets, Fluffy was living undercover because her owners didn't want to pay the $200 yearly pet fee the complex charged. They got away with it for most of the year but towards the end their luck ran out. Somehow the apartment management had learned about Fluffy and the guys received something that all students dread: a payment notice. It stated that they had never paid their pet fee and that is was due immediately. Jimmy was ready to write a check right away; after all they were caught red handed.

But lucky for him Clay was devious and had a few tricks up his sleeve. "We can get out of this," he said confidently. It turns out that their apartment complex had changed management three times over the last few months, and sometimes things get disorganized. This can work to a tenant's advantage if they know how to milk the system.

With the air of annoyance and a cocky swagger, Clay strolled into the office with the payment notice and declared, "I don't know what you're talking about. I already paid this." "Do you have a receipt?" asked the receptionist. "No, I paid it a long time ago. I don't have a receipt anymore." (What an actor.) "Ok, well we'll look for it and get back to you."

A few days went by and Clay received a phone call from the management. "Sir, we couldn't find any record of your $200 payment." A dramatic pause. Nice try, but games up right? No way, not for Clay, he held his ground of false deception. "Well, I'm not paying it again," he stated firmly. "And you know, you guys have changed management *three times* since I've lived here. You probably lost it." What's next, eviction? Court summons? No, they tucked their tail between their legs and gave in, "We're sorry for the inconvenience sir." Suckers.

Cat Woman

Most animal lovers will tell you that a pet is not just a possession, but a member of the family. There is usually a mutual bond of love and affection between humans and their pets. One can be willing to risk their life for the other. Ever watch those TV specials about people being saved from certain death by their dogs, cats, pigs, even birds? No doubt about it; people often grow very attached to their pets and will go to great lengths to care for and protect them.

There are times, however, when a love for pets can take on an unhealthy and psychotic twist, leaving friendships, valuables, and money in the dust. Such was the case for Sophie. She lived in a house off campus with two other girls, and one of them had her own cat, Garfield. Sophie loved

Garfield and decided that she too, wanted a cat. But one was not enough, so

she decided to get four kittens. That's right: four. Two for herself and two for

her fiancée who was backpacking in Europe; she wanted to surprise him with

them when he returned home. Welcome back honey, meow.

Sophie was definitely a prime example of someone who listened to her

heart more than her brain. She soon learned that kittens aren't just sweet little

fur balls that make cute posters; they are living, breathing things that require

certain necessities such as food, water, grooming, and litter. Well wouldn't you

know it, all that stuff costs money! Sophie barely had enough to pay the rent,

so she couldn't afford to buy them these essentials. Poor Garfield. His food

and litter box were soon taken over by these greedy little pussies.

Not only were they freeloaders, these kitties were also mini destroyers.

They spent their days clawing away at the furniture and drapes. And since

Sophie couldn't afford to declaw them, they were loaded with plenty of ammo.

The arrival of these precious bundles brought friction into their happy house.

Her roommates weren't pleased with their new housemates. They were now

buying twice as much food and litter as before and the couch was being

scratched to shreds. Time to say goodbye to the freeloading pussies.

When they confronted Sophie with their issues, she was appalled at the thought of getting rid of her beloved pets. They had become like children to her. *Children she didn't bother to feed.* Days went on of bickering back and forth, until finally they reached a compromise: Sophie could keep two of the cats, but the other two would have to go. This way it would be cheaper for her to support them.

Problem solved? No. It's never that simple when people aren't operating with a full deck. Once the landlord got wind of all the damage the cats had caused, he insisted she get rid of her last two. Of course Sophie wouldn't consider parting with them, so she came up with her own bizarre solution.

One day while Sophie was parking on campus, her friend Jill walked over to say hello, and was shocked to see two cats crawling over the steering wheel. "Sophie, why the heck do you have cats in your car?" she asked in disbelief. "The landlord won't let me have them in the house, so I have to keep them in here," Sophie answered nonchalantly. Oh my God, ever hear of a kennel? Her car had become sort of a jumbo-sized pet carrier, with the food and litter box kept in the back seat. This of course made the car smell heavenly. Poor kitties. If you were a cat, would you want to live in a car?

This odd arrangement went on for a few weeks, but soon Sophie felt sorry for her felines being so confined, so one day she tried sneaking them back into the house. Bad idea. While she was at class, the landlord just happened to show up that day to do some repairs. After he found the cats, he was livid. He put each of them in a cat carrier then sat in the kitchen and waited for Sophie to return. When Sophie came home, she was horrified at the "abuse" of her beloved pets. How dare he restrain them like that? *But keeping them in the car isn't abuse, right?* The result was a shouting match between her and the landlord:

"You fat asshole! You can't treat my cats like that!"

"I sure as hell can! This is the last straw! You've had enough warnings. Keep your damn cats away from the house or you're outta here!"

"You don't need to bother kicking me out because I'm leaving today!" Sophie yelled furiously.

Great comeback, except it wasn't too thought out. Sophie had no place to go and barely any money. Her mouth spoke before her brain could stop it, and her pride just wouldn't let her back down. What was a girl to do? Everybody needs friends, especially people whose lack of sense leads them to dig their own graves. Sophie called Jill, and asked her to come over right away. "I'll explain everything later, but please come over right now and bring your truck."

Jill had no idea what was going on, but when she pulled up behind Sophie's car she saw the two cats peering out of the back window and Sophie was frantically loading things into it. "I'm leaving today, so I need your truck to take my furniture to storage," Sophie explained as she shoved clothes into the front seat. Jill was in shock. This behavior was too crazy even by Sophie's standards. "Where are you gonna go?" She asked cautiously. *There was no way she was going to let Sophie stay with her, especially not with those stupid cats.*

"Haley said I could stay at her dorm," Sophie answered as she marched back and forth between the house and car. Now *that* sounded like a good arrangement. Haley lived in the freshmen dorms, which meant one bedroom for four people, and with Sophie that made five. Three weeks left in the semester, two cats, one car, no money, and a partridge in a pear tree. She got the car loaded in record time and Jill followed her to the storage unit. All the time thinking, "How the hell did I get dragged into this?"

Somehow Sophie managed to wean out the last few weeks at Haley's dorm. She even was able to swindle free meals from the cafeteria. The cats stayed in the car and she would routinely go out to visit and feed them. Poor pussies. Her money was almost gone, but she finally found a job as a cashier at Wal-Mart. So instead of going home for the summer, her plan was to stay at her friend Nikki's apartment. She wasn't on the lease, but she would be helping with rent, a common occurrence in college living.

But once again, the cats came into play. Although she was allergic to them, Nikki had the misjudgment of allowing Sophie to bring the cats inside; provided she kept them in her room. As it turned out, this wasn't a good arrangement. One day Sophie took off for a spur of the moment road trip without any warning. Apparently she thought the cats could fend for themselves, because she left them locked up in her room. Nikki wasn't about to care for them; her allergies would flare up.

The cats spent the week pissing and crapping all over the room, causing permanent damage to the carpet and the bed that Nikki had loaned her. This, of course, put a damper on their friendship. When Sophie returned she found a note from Nikki taped to the fridge, telling her that she had three days to move out of the apartment. Hey, at least Nikki didn't throw the cats out the window.

Think this was the end of Sophie's cat raid? No. For all her troubles this girl also had bouts of good luck, because once again a Good Samaritan came to her aid. Her friend Kyle offered to let her stay on his couch for the rest of the summer. This time, the cats stayed in the car. Although she wasn't paying rent, Kyle did get some perks out of it. Since the place was small and Sophie wasn't very modest, she would often change her clothes right in front of him. He would be pouring his coffee and turn around to see Sophie stripped to her underwear, a nice way for a guy to wake up in the morning.

At the end of the summer Sophie moved out of state to be with her boyfriend. And ...are you ready for this? She left the cats behind! She got kicked out of two places because of those damn cats and in the end decided she didn't want them! Too bad she didn't decide that a few months earlier, it would have saved her and her poor friends a lot of trouble.

As for the cats, they were given up to new home. After months of living in a car and sporadic feedings, it's doubtful they were too heartbroken over the separation. Hopefully, their new owner had more traditional methods of animal lodging, or else those cats would probably learn how to kill themselves from car exhaust.

Sexual Escapades

If someone never received sex education in high school, they will surely get it in college. A coed dorm can come to resemble a swingers' club. Put lots of young, single coeds together with raging hormones, no parental supervision, and easy access to alcohol and you just pray they know how to unroll a condom. Fortunately most campuses provide free condoms, so ladies don't fall for the old, "I can't afford them" line. They're free, use em'. Naturally, with the crowded living conditions a dorm often becomes like an Indian teepee. Ever seen "Dances With Wolves?" They just slept right through it while a couple bumped and grinded under the buffalo skin. Some people are going to have sex no matter who can see or hear it, and this can lead to some awkward situations.

Naked Intruder

"To sleep perchance to dream." -- (William Shakespeare's Hamlet)

Sleep is a time to escape the tension of the day and drift off into a quiet, darkened bliss. It's supposed to be a period free from annoying distractions, allowing the body and mind to rest and recharge. But there are always occasional night-time surprises. We've all had a few unwanted wake-ups in our life and in rare times they require police intervention.

April was in her junior year when she experienced something that would rouse the dead. One night after a few too many she decided to crash at her friend's sorority house. Curled up on the couch, she felt a tap on her shoulder and opened her eyes to see a naked guy standing over her. His tiny balls and hairy cock were illuminated in the moonlight; no wonder most people prefer sex in the dark.

Poor April was terrified. Was this a rapist or a burglar who was a really light dresser? She wasn't about to find out. Screaming frantically, she jumped up, ran upstairs, and dialed 911. "Help me, please! There's a naked guy here! I think he's going to kill me! HELP!" Her screams alerted the other girls in the house and within seconds everyone was screaming and running around wielding lamps and any other kind of make-shift weapon. April was hysterical and hard to understand so most of them had no idea what they were screaming about; it just seemed like the appropriate response. The cops arrived and found the nude bandit hiding in a closet. After some tough interrogation, the bandit was confessing his crime to the officers.

It turns out he was the one-night stand of one of the girls in the house. She brought him home from the bar and had her way with him. He must have been really bad in bed because when he got up to pee she locked him out of the bedroom, with all of his clothes still inside.

When it was apparent she wasn't going to let him back in, the naked Romeo decided to wake the girl on the couch to help him get his clothes back. *Lucky for him April wasn't armed with scissors.* This turned out to be a very embarrassing lay for all parties involved. The moral of the story is: don't get naked for sex; it's not worth the risk of arrest.

No Gum Chewing

We've all heard the phrase, "no gum chewing allowed" at certain times in our lives. While gum is a popular and simple amusement, its presence is not always appropriate. This was a common rule in the elementary years; the cracking and popping can be a distraction to learning. Not to mention the unsanitary methods of disposal, garbage cans are never as convenient as sticking it beneath a desk or chair. But as lewd as it is for someone to pin their

DNA wad on public property, there are some places that rate below humanity.

Paula discovered this during her sophomore year at Tramp University. A free spirited young woman with lack-luster hygiene, she soon gained a shameless reputation as being easy to lay and vile to smell. While she found time to sleep with a different guy almost every night, she only bathed about twice a week. Sweat and semen were more familiar to her than soap or water. Perhaps she thought the scent of cum would be a source of arousal.

One morning while preparing for a sporadic shower, Paula was busy filling her roommate Stacey in on her most recent sexual encounter from the night before. Another drunk guy she had stumbled home with (God knows what kind of sexual history or diseases he had). Poor Stacey listened patiently and was too polite to say she didn't want the daily whore report.

During the retelling Paula turned on the shower and stripped down to her underwear, all of a sudden showing a confused facial expression. Reaching down into her panties, she slowly pulled out a dried up yellow clump from her twat. "What's this?" she asked innocently.

It was one of those moments where you wished you could stop the clock and run out the door. There, straight from Paula's pussy, was gum. That's right, a chewed up, dried out, pre-sex breath-enhancer. Apparently the drunk bastard she had hooked up with blew it out while traveling south.

Maybe he thought it would freshen the smell?

While Stacey struggled to hold down her breakfast, Paula didn't seem the least bit phased by her vagina being used as a mini garbage can. She laughed, tossed it out, and proceeded to take a much needed dousing. Keep in mind this was her first washing since that sick encounter, makes you wonder if she had any other foreign objects hiding out inside her.

This story brings safe sex to an all new level. Rules for protected sex: 1: Use a condom. 2. Spit out your gum. While it's doubtful Paula always told a guy to use a condom, you can bet that from then on she made him toss his gum.

"False Identification"

Everyone varies in their attitude towards public sex. Some people are very open about it, willing to discuss experiences and display affection, while others are more conservative, believing sex should be kept behind closed doors so no one else can see or hear the bodies in motion. Of course if you go away to college, it can be all but impossible to keep sex hidden living in cramped conditions. Which is why if you want to have sex in the dorms, it helps to have a casual attitude about it.

Amanda was just that type of person. She came to college with a free-spirit mind set and often described her sexual escapades with no fear or shame: "Yeah, Matt and I went at it for hours last night. He was so drunk he couldn't finish, so I finally told him to stop cause my crotch was drying up." Not exactly dinner conversation, but at least her stories offered free entertainment.

Hard to believe, but Amanda actually managed to have sex more than she talked about it. A self-proclaimed nymphomaniac, Amanda would often skip aerobics class to perform her own private workout. Lucky for her, her boyfriend Matt also had a raging sex drive, so he was able to keep up with Amanda's sensuous cravings.

They could be heard at all hours of the day driving the headboard into the wall, making it sound as if the Earth was shaking. Amanda's roommate Jamie wasn't bothered by her sexual habits. With all her talk and noise, Amanda was considerate enough to wait until Jamie left the room before embarking on another mattress test. This kept them living in a peaceful setting.

One thing about Matt was that he was short, thin, and had long, wavy hair. He was cute, but definitely not manly, and from the back he was often mistaken for a girl. Amanda didn't mind, because as she put it: "It's not how big a man is, it's how he uses what he's got. And trust me, that boy's got it." Little did she know that Matt's small stature would soon lead to a very awkward encounter.

One day Amanda and Matt were going at it in the middle of the afternoon, when the unsuspecting Jamie got home early from class. The radio was on, so she didn't hear the raunchy sounds coming from the bedroom. Amanda heard Jamie start squawking, "Oh my God! Oh my God!" Then the door slammed behind her.

Later on, Amanda tried joking with her about it, "So what'd you'd think of seeing me in action?" But Jamie wouldn't even look at her; she just lowered her head and scurried away. "Maybe she's just embarrassed," Amanda thought. At first she wasn't too concerned, thinking Jamie just needed time to get over it. But this went on for several days, with Jamie acting as if Amanda had the plague. Finally, after spending a good part of the week in silence, Jamie spoke up:

"There's something I have to talk to you about." "OK, what's going on?" Amanda was relieved to hear her roommate speak to her again. "I just want you to know that however you choose to live your life is your business, but I really don't think you're being fair to Matt. He deserves to know the truth. And I'm not going to cover for you."

Amanda was dumbfounded. This certainly wasn't what she expected to hear. Something more along the lines of, "Could you please leave a, "Do Not

Disturb" sign up the next time you have sex?" Not knowing how to respond, she just sat and waited. "I don't care who you sleep with. But if you're going to have a relationship with Jessica then you shouldn't be with Matt."

Amanda thought her ears were deceiving her. "What the hell are you talking about?" she demanded. *Jessica was her friend who lived down the hall.* "I'm talking about when I walked in on you and Jessica in bed. Don't deny it; I know you heard me slam the door." "What! That wasn't Jessica, that was Matt!" Amanda exclaimed as she burst out laughing. Man, this was one for the books. What a case of mistaken identity. Poor Matt. Someone saw him naked and they still thought he was a female! "Oh, well, with his long hair and all, I guess I just got confused. Sorry." Jamie said sheepishly.

Mystery solved. Now that she knew her roommate was not having a lesbian affair, everything returned to normal. As for Matt, he was greatly embarrassed when Amanda shared the story with him. Who wouldn't be, really? Although he couldn't do much about his small body, he did go out and get a haircut right away, claiming he was sick of styling it all the time. Coincidence? What do you think?

Great Immunity

Everyone varies in the number of sexual partners that they've had. Some remain virgins till death, marriage, while others seek to make a new world record. No matter who you sleep with, you're probably also sleeping with their past mates. Example: Suzy is a virgin when she sleeps with Mike, but Mike has slept with three girls before her, and between the three of them they have been with a total of 8 guys.

So Suzy is not just sleeping with Mike for her first time, she is also sleeping with 11 other people. That's a lot to handle at once in bed. Let's just hope these people knew the importance of protection. According to the U.S. Centers for Disease Control, Condoms are 98% effective when used correctly. Unfortunately, just because someone had the brains to get into college doesn't mean they are smart enough to have safe sex.

Jackie witnessed this personally during her freshmen year. It didn't take long to realize that her roommate, Katie, didn't come to school for academics. She made it clear that she wanted to get as much dick as possible. The first night they moved in the dorm Katie brought some random guy home from a party, keeping Jackie up half the night with her moaning and banging.

That was just the beginning of her sexual frenzy. Katie had a goal to get as much sex as she could, and she brought random guys back almost every day. Too bad she wasn't majoring in whore studies. With all this action going on you'd think there'd be some condom wrappers left around, but Jackie never saw one, not even in the garbage.

After a few weeks she got up the courage to ask Katie about this. "Katie, have you been using protection with any of these guys?" Katie's response, "No, I never do. I'm on the pill." "Well, aren't you worried you'll get diseases? I mean the pill won't protect you from that." Brace yourself for this one: "Naw, I've got a good immune system." And she was serious. Who knows where she got that information, but your immune system cannot stop you from catching sexual diseases. Jackie tried explaining this to her slut roommate, but it fell on deaf ears.

As for Katie, she continued her sexual attack on campus until the end of the semester. After that she moved home because she was failing every class, what a surprise. God knows how many diseases she caught or gave. Jackie was grateful she wasn't a guy, or else she might have fallen prey to Katie's treacherous pussy. So a word to the wise: if you're going to fool around in the rain, make sure you wear your rubbers.

Vaginal Bacon

It is a common fact that bad hygiene can lead to foul odors and social isolation. After all, no one wants to be around anyone who smells bad. It is uncomfortable and annoying, wearing away at your patience and sanity. In some rare cases, one's hygiene can even become a danger to those around them. This is exactly what Amelia discovered during her freshmen year at college, as she became familiar with the term, "vaginal bacon."

Her roommate, Becca, was a coed that was a little odd in the sense that she seemed to have no need for cleanliness or privacy. She only showered every few days, so her hair was often limp and greasy. She loved discussing her sexual escapades, and whenever her boyfriend would come over, she would always recant to them about what they did and how long it lasted. "It took him so long to cum, I thought my arm was going to break off," she would casually mention while they were watching TV or eating a meal. Amelia and the others never wanted to hear the dirty details, but they put up with it. It became sort of a joke among them. "How long did he last this time?" Little did they know just how "dirty" Becca's details could get…

One evening her man came over and they went in her room for a romp. This was a common occurrence so the other roommates continued to chat in the living area and didn't think anything of it. A few minutes later, the guy rushed out of the room holding his hand over his eye. He took off down the hall and Becca casually strolled out after him. "This sucks, he was eating me out so good and he had to stop!" she moaned as she plopped down on the sofa.

Thankfully her shorts were back on. "Becca, what's going on? Why did he leave holding his eye?" "While he was sucking on me, something flew up from my crotch and hit him in the eye," Becca answered, all the while looking as if she was merely telling the weather forecast. "I don't know what it was, something black, maybe some knotted pubes or something."

Who can say a phrase like "knotted pubes" and still keep a straight face? Becca was either a great actor or a total nut; and the girls weren't sure which. Becca went back into her room and they sat there in bewilderment and disgust. It wasn't too long before her roommates had their own encounter with Becca's *vaginal bacon.* A few days after the eye incident, they found a small black leafy substance next to Becca's bed. Let's see...small and black, matches the description, found at the scene of the crime...it had to be...VAGINAL BACON!

Overcome with both laughter and nausea, they rounded up people in the hall to come and see! Fortunately Becca was at class, but who knows, she might have been proud of it. From then on Becca was known as "VP" (vaginal bacon.) She didn't seem to mind. Her showering habits did not improve, and her roommates carefully wore something on their feet at all times. They didn't want to get any *bacon* between the toes. As for the victim, he survived his bacon attack, but not before making a trip to the campus health center and getting it removed. How did he explain that one to the doctors? He and Becca continued having their graphic sex. Strangely though, for some reason Becca now kept a pair of goggles next to her bed.

Chlamydia Chick

Most of us are familiar with the phrase, *practice what you preach*. It is a simple saying with a strong noble standing. You can't just talk about good morals; you need to exhibit them. Unfortunately, many people can talk the talk but end up skipping the walk. We all know that actions speak louder than words, and in some cases, they scream in sexual ecstasy.

Rhonda had such an experience during her sophomore year. Her roommate, Wendy, was known as one of the campus *preachers*. She was heavily involved with one of the Christian groups on campus and spent a lot her free time reading the Bible, praying out loud, and meditating.
She always wore a cross around her neck and a W.W.J.D (What Would Jesus Do?) bracelet.

From the outside she was an exemplary role model of a devout Christian and at first Rhonda was impressed by Wendy's devotion. So when Wendy told her she was going to start leading a weekly prayer group in their room, Rhonda had no objections. At least it wasn't a drinking fest where she would have to worry about beer stains or puke. Hey, maybe she could benefit from it, too.

"Would it be all right if I came?" she asked. "Praise Jesus! God welcomes everyone to join in worship!" Wendy replied with a big smile. Later that week several bible-toting students showed up at their doorway. "Welcome to university prayer!" Wendy exclaimed as she let them in. After a few minutes of hugging and greeting, Wendy turned off the lights, lit a few candles, and they all sat in a circle and held hands. Rhonda was curious to see how things would unfold.

After about 20 minutes of group prayer, Wendy opened her bible. "The topic of our session tonight is abstinence," she announced in a serious tone. "Was it my imagination or did she look at me when she said that?" Rhonda thought, instantly feeling uneasy. She wondered if this was some sort of a set-up. Her mind flashed back to earlier in the semester, when she had made the mistake of telling Wendy that she was not a virgin. "God forgives all sins, but you should repent," Wendy had told her.

Rhonda took a deep breath and braced herself for a lecture. "Today we live in a society where it is considered acceptable to have pre-marital intercourse. But let me tell you something, despite what you might hear and see, it is not acceptable. The Lord says we must wait until marriage before having sexual relations."

Rhonda glanced around and wondered if she was the only non-virgin in the room. She felt like leaving, but didn't want to seem like a bible-bashing bitch. Gritting her teeth, she grimaced as Wendy went on and on about the evils of sex before marriage. Mercifully, after a few rounds of hugging and farewells, the session finally ended. Feeling a bit insulted; Rhonda immediately went for a walk. "Who does she think she is, judging me like that?" she mumbled to herself. The whole time she had felt like a spotlight was on her, a light of cherry-popped shame.

When she returned an hour later, Rhonda was surprised to find the lights were still off and their bedroom door was shut. She was about to open it when she heard some strange sounds coming from within, squeaking bedsprings and low moans and giggles. What's going on? Was this another type of prayer session? Not wanting to intrude, Rhonda sat down and flipped on the TV. She didn't have to wait long.

After few minutes the door opened and Wendy came out with some unknown guy who she introduced as "Tim." "Bye sweetie, I'll see you tomorrow," she said as he walked out. "Wendy, what's the deal with all that abstinence shit? I heard you fucking that guy! Where do you get off lecturing me about it?" Rhonda exclaimed in shock. She was too nice; she should have walked in while they were going at and started reading the bible.

"I'd appreciate it if you referred to it as "lovemaking" not "fucking." Wendy replied. She didn't seem the least bit embarrassed or ashamed for being caught, "in the act." "I am not breaking any of rules. As long as I pray, God will restore my virginity." She was dead serious. Rhonda couldn't believe her ears. This was only the beginning of Wendy's quest to lose and *regain* her flowerhood. The weekly bible sessions continued with Tim coming over after each session for a private bodily worship.

It turns out that Wendy also had a big appreciation for our troops. Wanting to do her own part to support the armed forces, one day she brought a soldier home who was about to be shipped overseas.

He must have wanted to leave her something to remember him by, because she got a nice case of Chlamydia afterwards. Maybe she had thought that God would also *shield* her in bed. What was a girl to do? Tim would surely dump her if he learned the truth and that would put an end to their post-bible banging, so she told him she got it because she had been raped at a party. No joke. Isn't that sick? That made her both a hypocrite and a liar.

This was all too much for Rhonda; her roommate was a deceitful sermon-slut. Needless to say, that first prayer session was the only one she went to. She still followed God, just not with Wendy. From then on she referred to her as *Chlamydia Chick*. Chlamydia *lost* and *regained* her virginity dozens of times that year, while continuing to preach abstinence at her prayer sessions. Let's just hope this girl doesn't end up leading a cult one-day, it could create a new society of *virgin* tramps.

Time for a Spanking

We all have heard stories of girls being used for sex. They are often warned from an early age to be cautious of male predators. "Remember, guys just want one thing." Men are often portrayed as scum who will say or do anything just to get a piece of ass: "Of course I'll still respect you," "I really care about you," or "I would never use you, baby." While it's true that certain men deserve such a reputation, some poor guys find themselves at the receiving end of sexual conquests.

During her freshmen year, Olivia was a pretty skank who loved to prey on dumb young men. She would convince them she liked them, earn their trust, string them along .... and then break their hearts! "Fuck em' then dump em' was her motto. Not exactly a girl with high moral standards.

One day she brought an unsuspecting victim, Larry, over to her dorm. When they walked in her roommates were watching TV. Olivia told Larry to go into the bedroom and wait for her, then she turned and announced to everyone, "Watch out guys, I'm about to have sex and I'll try to make you all laugh."

She went into the bedroom, closed the door, and within minutes the whole hall heard her screaming at him, "Oh baby! Give it to me! Give it to me! Harder...yes! Right there...that's the spot!" Spanking him: smack! smack! smack! "How's that feel? You want some more? I'm going to make your ass pink! Now bend me over baby! Bend me over! Hey you're pretty small. You know what I'll call you? Little Larry! Oh, oh, yes! Give it to me Little Larry!"

Needless to say, everyone who heard was rolling around with laughter. Lucky for Larry there wasn't a video camera in the room. This explosive sex concert went on for a good twenty minutes. Olivia had a strong set of lungs to keep that up. When Larry emerged and saw everyone laughing at him, he hung his head and did the *walk of shame*.

"Well ladies, did you get a kick out of that or what?" Olivia said as she came out wrapped in a sheet. "Didn't he know we could hear you?" they

129

asked "Oh yeah, but I told him he couldn't stop or else I'd tell everyone he was bad in bed," Olivia said smugly. Smart ploy, but what a bitch!

Poor Larry. From then on whenever they ran into him on campus, Olivia would scream, "Hey Little Larry!" This is how she referred to him for the rest of their college career. He never lived it down. Hopefully he learned a valuable lesson: be very mindful of who you sleep with, or you can end up doing the "walk of shame" in front of a laughing audience.

Can't Suck This

One of the great things about college life is the diversity among the students. On most campuses, students make up a wide population of different cultures, races, religions, ethnicity, backgrounds, body mass, and of course: sexual orientation. The typical Liberal atmosphere on campus makes it much easier for most students to come out of the closet in college rather than in high school. This is a wonderful thing because they can finally open up and express who they really are, but occasionally self-expression can go too far.

Shawna had such an experience during her freshmen year. After growing up in a small-town with a sheltered childhood, she was craving for fresh experiences at college. On move-in day she met her roommate, Leah, for the first time. Leah wasn't the type of person you "wondered" about. With her baggy jeans, cropped hair, backward cap and rainbow necklace, she could have been a poster child for gay rights. In fact one of the first things she said after introducing herself was, "Just so you know, I'm gay." This didn't really bother Shawna. After all, she wasn't a judgmental person. And part of college was accepting differences right? Unfortunately, some things just aren't acceptable.

Leah had a girlfriend Sam, and those two had no shame about showing their passion in public. They didn't believe in private affection and would put on shows for anyone who was around. They would make out with the door open while the guys across the hall cheered them on "Yeah, baby! Eat them flaps!" And have loud, moaning showers together whenever Shawna was home.

OK, definitely not something she was used to, but Shawna kept an open mind and tried to ignore the constant taco eating. One afternoon she ended up taking a nap on the couch, and found herself having a bizarre dream that a dog was licking her toes. She woke up with a jolt.

A dog *was sucking* on her feet, but it wasn't the kind with four legs. Sam was crouched at the end of the couch, head bent down, devouring her toes like a cat goes for tuna. Did they taste better than Leah's lips?

Needless to say, this was not a time for a subtle response. Shawna did not appreciate having her feet molested. "What the fuck are you doing! Are you crazy! Get the hell away from me!" *Perhaps she was slightly aroused and afraid to admit it.* This little piggy went to market, this little piggy stayed home, and this little piggy got frenched.

When Shawna told Leah what happened, she didn't understand what the big deal was. Sam was only playing around, she claimed, no harm done. But in order to keep the peace, she agreed to cut back on their public sex shows and make sure Sam's tongue was only reserved for her pleasure.

Shawna managed to survive the rest of the school year, but from then on she never slept without her socks on.

Masturbation

By the time one enters college they have had plenty of time to become seasoned masturbators. Puberty is over, and they are usually well aware of how their body functions and what it takes to produce sexual satisfaction. With all of the raging hormones on campus, masturbation is a quick, simple, and safe way to relieve carnal urges. Of course not everyone has mastered the art of being discreet about their solo sex acts, and this can lead to some very discomforting roommate encounters.

Main Entry: mas·turba·tion Function: noun: erotic stimulation especially of one's own genital organs commonly resulting in orgasm and achieved by manual or other bodily contact exclusive of sexual intercourse, by instrumental manipulation, occasionally by sexual fantasies, or by various combinations of these agencies.

-Merriam Webster Internet Dictionary

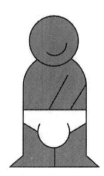

Web Entertainment

As technology continues to improve, communication is becoming more and more accessible. Voicemail, text messaging, Facebook, and online chat are all quick and easy ways to get in touch with people. No matter how far apart you are, communication can be right at your disposable, and with the invention of the web cam it is now possible to see people while you shoot the shit. This is all fun and innocent, but there are always ways to embody X-rated behavior; remember American Pie? Sometimes private acts aren't always hidden. When you come home unexpectedly, you can sometimes catch your roommates in awkward situations.

Come on, we all do things alone that we wouldn't do in front of others. With the roommates out it can make for a good study session or a nice scratch and touch yourself time. Rita learned this during her freshmen year. Her roommate, Laura, was one of the many students who spent most of her waking hours in front of the computer. She would often skip class to surf the Internet and play in chat rooms, using her web cam to check out the guys online. Nothing wrong with that, right? But it turns out that Laura had her own erotic methods of getting attention.

One afternoon Rita's class got canceled, so she came back early. When she opened the door she was shocked at what she found: Laura was standing in front of her webcam, pants around her ankles, masturbating. That's right: masturbating, the safest and easiest form of sexual pleasure. No partner or protection necessary.

Now Rita had nothing against her roommate performing self-satisfaction. After all, studies show that it helps relieve menstrual cramps, insomnia, and stimulates the immune system. What she *did have* a problem with was walking in during the middle of it. It put an image in her mind that she'll have to live with the rest of her life, unless she gets blessed with amnesia later on.

Lucky for Rita, Laura was a considerate Internet slut. She agreed to refrain from such behavior unless it was guaranteed that Rita would be gone for a while. (Going to class didn't count.) Hey, it could have been worse; at least Laura didn't ask her to join in. They lived out the rest of the semester in peace, with Rita becoming notorious for knocking before entering. Better safe than sorry. Maybe that was why Laura chose that method of pleasure instead of finding a partner. It's pretty hard to get pregnant through a web cam.

Bottoms Up

We've all heard stories about sex in the shower. It's the perfect environment for doing the deed because you're already naked, everything stays wet, and you're clean when you finish. It's an easy way to kill two birds with one stone. *Or pop two cherries.* A good friend of mine once said, *"The best way to have sex is to start out clean, and end dirty."* What a wonder the shower hasn't taken over for the world's most popular breeding ground. You start out clean, and end clean too!

Lenny was a typical twenty-something guy who enjoyed sex anywhere he could get it. Indoors, outdoors, wet, dry, dirty, clean, whatever and wherever it didn't matter to him. As long as there was some vodka in his system anyplace was fair game to get laid. He and his girlfriend Mimi had been dating for over three years, and after so much time together they had passed the original excitement of sex. The novelty had worn off for Mimi and poor Lenny sometimes had to beg to get any action. Hey, it's better than having to pay.

One evening they had plans to go out to a party. Lenny decided to pre-drink with multiple shots of vodka while his sweetie fretted over what to wear. When she finally made it to the shower Lenny was wasted and ready to hit it up. He surprised her while she was shaving her legs and tried to land his target, but his women was not about to choose drunken sex over smooth skin. She pushed him away and continued to groom.

Not about to be shut down, Lenny declares, "I can do it better myself!" He grabs his masculinity and starts to jerk off to high heaven. Mimi laughs as he closes his eyes and starts to lose himself in the moment. Holding onto to the curtain for balance, he leans back to sink into ultimate pleasure. Unfortunately the shower curtain wasn't as strong as he thought; and before he could shoot his load Lenny fell out of the shower and took the rod with him, crashing onto his behind.

Mimi screamed, fearing he had broken has back. A brief pause after the shock of the fall; then suddenly Lenny grimaces in pain; "My ass! My ass!" he moaned. He rolled over and saw what no man should ever witness: a shampoo bottle was sticking out of his rectum. Lenny felt as if he had just been taken as a prison wife.

He reached behind him and pulled it from his ass. The cap was bloody and made a slight suction noise from extraction. *Ouch.* Poor Lenny. Maybe his subconscious was trying to tell him something, because his ass had no problem finding its target. After rubbing on some Neosporin he was as good as new, but from then on no more shower sex.

Please Clean That

As a first year RA, Taylor knew she was bound to encounter some new experiences. She lived in a coed freshmen dorm, so her residents were all fresh out of mom and dad's house, eager for freedom with their hormones raging. The university had put her through weeks of training in order to be prepared for this job, reenacting many possible problems and roommate scenarios. But as we all know, there are some things you just can't be ready for.

It all began as a typical weeknight in the dorms. Nothing out of the ordinary had happened that day and Taylor was hoping for some uninterrupted study time. She was in the middle of some fascinating psychology when two of her residents, Nate and Logan, came down to her room. "We've got a problem and we need your help," they said.

Upon hearing this, Taylor was expecting the usual freshmen roommate dilemmas: poor hygiene? Lack of cleaning? Missing food? Come on...bring it! She didn't get this job for nothing! She was there to help her residents solve their conflicts in a peaceful manner.

It turned out these guys had both a unique and disgusting problem. Their roommate, Josh, was frequently masturbating in the shower. How did they know this? He always left his jizz on the wall for the next lucky bather. Maybe he was trying to show off his shooting range or perhaps he couldn't think straight after cumming. For whatever the reason, Josh never cleaned up after blowing his load, and it was driving his roommates crazy.

Wow! There sure was nothing in the RA manual for this situation. How was she going to handle this one? This called for a ...drum roll please ...ROOMMATE NEGOTIATION!   No time to waste in this situation, with all the fun he had in the shower, Josh was compelled to keep up his daily bathing.

She met with all the guys that same night and surprisingly, it was a rather quick and easy resolution. Josh claimed he had no idea that his habit bothered anyone, and he agreed to clean up the mess from then on. Voila! Problem solved. It was never an issue again. Thank-God for open communication. Let's just hope Josh never took a special liking to shampoo bottles.

Final Notes

Despite all of the shocking stories in this book, I still believe having roommates is an important life experience. Some of my fondest memories of college aren't the wild parties or football games, but everyday roommate bonding such as ordering late-night pizza or having bunk bed chats. Coming from someone who had lived with thirty-nine different people in college, it teaches you how to tolerate many types of personalities and confront touchy situations. Since you are dealing with roommates you can't go home and escape your problem for a while. This forces people to confront things they normally would avoid. Growing up, I was never one to confront anybody, always trying to ignore people I didn't like. But college forced me to learn my boundaries and how to assert myself. When you're living under the same roof with difficult people you're backed into a corner. That leaves you with two choices; either speak up or curl into submission. You learn a lot about yourself; how your habits affect others and what makes you tick. Best of all, it shares the vital message that living alone is highly underrated.

The End

32958329R00081

Made in the USA
Lexington, KY
07 June 2014